STOP

Messing Around

How to Get Things Done and Crush Your Goals

M.G. David

DEDICATION

To you reading this book, wanting to stop messing around. Thank you.

CONTENTS

Conclusion 109

Personal Letter from Me to You

Dear Friend,

Congratulations! You've managed to stumble upon the solution to all your procrastination problems: "Stop Messing Around: How to get things done and crush your goals." I promise you, this book is going to change your life. Okay, maybe that's a bit dramatic, but it will definitely help you crush your goals and beat procrastination.

Now, before you start rolling your eyes and thinking, "Here we go again, another self-help book that's going to be boring and useless," hear me out. This book is different. It's written specifically for teens like you, with all your unique challenges and distractions.

Inside these pages, you'll find practical tips and tricks for getting things done, even when you'd rather be scrolling through TikTok or playing video games. You'll learn how to set goals, make a plan, and actually follow through on your commitments.

But here's the thing: you have to commit to reading the book and following the steps. It's not enough to just skim through the pages and then toss it aside. You have to be willing to put in the work and make a real effort to change your procrastinating ways.

That's where your accountability partner comes in. Find someone who will hold you accountable and keep you on track. Maybe it's a parent, a teacher, or a friend. They'll sign a little contract in the next letter committing to verify at the end that you've completed it and made progress in beating procrastination. Trust me, having someone in your corner can make all the difference. So, give whoever you've chosen the next letter

So, what do you say? Are you ready to stop messing around and start crushing your goals? I thought so. Get ready to take on the world, one task at a time.

Sincerely,
Michael G. David

Letter to Your Accountability Partner

Dear Accountability Partner,

I hope this letter finds you well. As you may already know, your teen has embarked on a journey to overcome procrastination by reading "Stop Messing Around: How to get things done and crush your goals." I'm writing to encourage you to support them on this journey and to commit to rewarding them with a surprise upon successfully implementing the principles in the book.

As an accountability partner, you play a critical role in helping your teen beat procrastination. Your support, encouragement, and guidance can make all the difference in helping them stay on track and make real progress. And what better way to motivate them than with a surprise reward?

The surprise doesn't have to be anything extravagant or expensive, but it should be something that your teen will appreciate and find motivating. It could be something as simple as a favorite treat or a fun outing, or something bigger like a new gadget or a special experience. Whatever it is, make sure it's something that will inspire them to keep going and make real progress.

When your teen successfully implements the principles in the book and completes their goals, it will be a big accomplishment. They'll have overcome one of the biggest challenges that many people face, and they'll be well on their way to achieving their dreams. And your support and encouragement will have played a big part in making that happen.

So, what do you say? Will you commit to rewarding your teen with a surprise upon successful implementation of the principles in the book? It may be just the extra motivation they need to stay focused and committed.

Thank you for your support, and I wish you and your teen all the best on this journey.

Sincerely,
Michael G. David

INTRODUCTION

Hey, teens! Let's talk about how our actions (or lack of actions) define who we are. You know that feeling when you look back and think, "Why didn't I do that thing?" It's like a heavy weight on your shoulders, right? And if you ask yourself, "What did I do instead?" and the answer is "Nothing useful," well, that's just a bummer.

Procrastination is the enemy of progress, my friends. It's held back so many people, killed careers and businesses, and even made people sick. That's why we got to learn to conquer it! And if you're holding this book, it means you're ready to kick some procrastination butt.

But let me tell you, reading this book is just the first step. You got to be serious about taking action too. Success is all about taking the right steps in the right order. And to do that, you got to know your enemy. Procrastination can be a sneaky one, so we got to get to know it really well to beat it.

I've struggled with procrastination too, and I tried everything from motivation to therapy. But my "aha" moment came when I realized I needed to understand it better. And now, I want to share all that knowledge with you. This book is full of simple tools based on solid research that have been proven to work. Trust me, they worked for me and for many others too. So, let's conquer procrastination and achieve greatness together!

PART 1
The More You Mess Around the More You Find Out

Hey there, my dudes and dudettes! Buckle up because we're about to learn a valuable lesson: messing around can have some serious consequences. But don't worry, it's not all doom and gloom! Despite these consequences, lots of folks have managed to bounce back and achieve greatness.

Chapter 1
IT IS REAL - MESSING AROUND HAS CONSEQUENCES

"Think of your many years of procrastination; how the gods have repeatedly granted you further periods of grace, of which you have taken no advantage. It is time now to realize the nature of the universe to which you belong, and of that controlling Power whose offspring you are and to understand that your time has a limit set to it. Use it, then, to advance your enlightenment; or it will be gone, and never in your power again."
Marcus Aurelius (121-180AD)

You **Don't Have All the Time.** Hey there, how much time do you think you've got? I'm not talking about your lifespan, no need to worry about that! I'm talking about the time you have, to make things happen. You only have 24 hours in a day, and you can't stretch it any further. You can't press pause to goof around and come back to it later, unfortunately. Time is like currency, and you've got to spend it wisely.

Think of it this way: every morning you wake up with 24 hours in your wallet. Every action you take throughout the day costs you some of that time. From sleeping to working, to eating and hanging out with friends, everything costs you time. And once you've spent it, you can't get it back.

So, what are you spending your time on? Studies show that students like you spend as much as 10 hours a day on social media and only 3.9 hours studying! Yikes! That's a lot of time spent on one thing.[1,2]

The good news is that you can reallocate your time to focus on what's important to you. If you have a goal you want to achieve, you'll need to make time for it. That means cutting back on other things or dropping them altogether.

But here's the thing: what you spend your time on will determine your value, happiness, and even your health. So, choose wisely and don't goof around. Procrastination is just another form of goofing around, so don't let it get the best of you. Spend your time on actions that will give you the highest value, whether it's eating healthy or working on a project that could pay off in the future.

Others Are Doing It..Why Shouldn't I

Have you ever noticed that sometimes you act totally irrational and do things that contradict what you know you should be doing? Like, you have a big project due or a test to study for, but instead of working on it, you find yourself scrolling through social media or binge-watching your favorite show. Well, you're not alone! Procrastination is a common problem that affects a lot of us.

But did you know that procrastination can actually have serious consequences? It can lead to missed opportunities, ruined relationships, and even physical health problems like heart disease! And despite all the studies and research out there, it seems like procrastination just keeps getting worse.[3,4,5]

But don't worry, there are ways to overcome procrastination! We just need to find unique approaches that work for us as individuals. So next time you catch yourself putting things off, try to take action right away, break your tasks into smaller, more manageable chunks, and eliminate any distractions that might be tempting you away from your goals.

Together, we can beat procrastination and achieve our dreams!

It's Been Around

Let's talk more about procrastination. You might think it's a new thing, but nope, it's been around for a hot minute. And guess what? It's only getting worse as technology makes it easier to do things from wherever you are. I mean, come on, who wants to do homework when you can binge-watch your favorite show on Netflix? But here's the kicker: procrastination has been a problem since ancient times, when people first started working together in groups. Back then, if someone slacked off on their part of a project, it could put the whole community in danger. And even the fancy-pants aristocrats and philosophers knew procrastination was a big deal. They wrote about it, warned against it, and even punished people for it.[6,7,8,9] But did that stop people from putting things off? Nope, not really. So, why is procrastination still a thing? That's the million-dollar question.

Dangers Of Messing Around

So, it's been around forever because it's just too dang easy to get sucked into doing something fun instead of what we should be doing. And let's be real, social media and internet surfing are just too tempting to resist sometimes. But here's the thing, procrastination is like a wolf in sheep's clothing. It might seem harmless and fun, but it can actually have some serious consequences.

Sure, we like to talk about how we can still get things done even if we procrastinate, but let's face it, that's not always the case. Research shows that procrastination is pretty harmful and can lead to all kinds of bad stuff like stress, anxiety, and even failure.[10,11] And let's not forget about the under-performance and low self-esteem that come with it.

One reason we procrastinate is because we underestimate how long it takes to get stuff done. And when unexpected problems arise, which they always do, we're left scrambling at the last minute and end up with poor performance or even failure. Plus, we always fall for the short-term benefits of procrastination, but in the long run, it can lead to mediocrity, misery, and poverty.

And if that's not enough to convince you to kick the procrastination habit, think about all the missed opportunities that come with putting things off. Time is a valuable thing, and when we waste it by messing around, we're essentially robbing ourselves of the chance to achieve our goals and dreams.

So, let's all try to be a little less like procrastinating sloths and a little more like productive unicorns. Trust me, it'll be worth it in the end!

Bad Endings

Hey, so have you ever seen your friends or family put things off until the last minute? Yeah, we've all been there. But have you ever thought about the serious consequences that can come from procrastination? I mean, it's not just about getting a bad grade or missing a deadline. It can hold you back from achieving your full potential!

I know, you've probably heard a million times from old people about how procrastination is bad, but I'm not here to lecture you. I'm just saying, let's take a look at some real-life examples of what can happen when you let procrastination take over.

Like this German colonel, John Rall, who was so distracted by a game that he didn't read a note that could have saved his life and his soldiers' lives.[12] Or General McClellan, who missed out on opportunities to win battles because he was too busy being meticulous.[13] And even Leonardo da Vinci, the genius himself, who couldn't finish anything on time because he was always daydreaming.[14,15]

But don't worry, it's not all doom and gloom. We can learn from these examples and take action to overcome procrastination. It might seem like a big deal, but trust me, even small actions can make a huge difference.

So, how can we do it? Well, we'll learn from John, Wendy, Ben, Linda, and Smith as they tackle their own procrastination problems. And we'll also look at some people who successfully beat procrastination, like Richard Sheridan, who even finished writing a play while it was already being performed on stage!

But here's the thing, reading this book alone won't solve your procrastination problems. You got to take action, even if it feels like a big step or a small one. Because in the end, taking action is the only way to overcome procrastination and achieve your goals. Are you ready to take that step?

So, take a sec to think about all the times you've left stuff until the eleventh hour and ended up stressing out, rushing to finish, or even straight up failing. Yeah, not cool. But hey, the good news is that recognizing the negative effects of procrastination is the first step in kicking the habit to the curb!

So, here are 5 things you've probably already experienced from putting things off:

1. The dreaded all-nighter: You know the feeling - it's 3am, you're chugging energy drinks and praying for a miracle just to finish that project you've had weeks to work on.
2. Stress levels through the roof: Waiting until the last minute can leave you feeling like you're running a marathon with no end in sight. Your stress levels skyrocket, and suddenly every little thing feels like a massive hurdle.
3. Quality suffers: When you rush through things, you're bound to make mistakes. Maybe you forgot to double-check your work, or maybe you didn't have time to give it your all. Whatever the case, your procrastination can seriously impact the quality of your work.
4. Regret city: Ever had that sinking feeling in your gut when you

realize you could have done so much better if you'd just started earlier? Yeah, it's not a fun place to be. Don't let procrastination be the cause of your regrets.

5. Missed opportunities: Last but not least, procrastination can cause you to miss out on some seriously cool opportunities. Maybe you didn't have time to apply for that dream internship, or maybe you missed the chance to impress your crush with your wicked guitar skills. Either way, putting things off can close doors you didn't even know were open.

These are examples and your experience may be a bit different. It is important to capture your own experience. So, answer the questions in the form below.

Me:

1. You must have noticed that procrastination is messing with your life. List the top 5 negative consequences you have experienced as a result of procrastinating.

   1. --
   2. --
   3. --
   4. --
   5. --

2. How do you think putting things off will make your life even worse? List the top 5 the negative consequences you're afraid might happen.

   1. --
   2. --
   3. --
   4. --
   5. --

Chapter 2
Its Antecedents - But You Can Still Break Free: Quitting's on the Table!

"We all sorely complain of the shortness of time, and yet have much more than we know what to do with. Our lives are either spent in doing nothing at all, or in doing nothing to the purpose, or in doing nothing that we ought to do. We are always complaining that our days are few and acting as though there would be no end of them."

Lucius Annaeus Seneca (4 BC – AD 65)

You **Can Choose to Stop.** Listen up, teens! We all know how tempting it is to put things off and just fool around instead. But if you want to stop procrastinating and get stuff done, you got to take action! Sounds easy enough, right? Well, not so fast. Your brain has this sneaky way of remembering the past and worrying about the future, which takes away from your "now time" and makes it hard to get stuff done in the present. It's like your brain is playing a mean trick on you!

So, what's the secret to beating procrastination? You got to live in the present, my friends. And to do that, you got to make a conscious choice to focus on the here and now. It's all about making that choice more attractive than dwelling on the past or stressing about the future. But let's be real, making that choice isn't always easy. It takes some serious willpower! But trust me, once you start living in the present and taking action, you'll be unstoppable. So, make that choice and go kick some butt!

It's Possible

Have you heard of these famous writers who were also notorious procrastinators? It's true, even successful people can struggle with getting started on their work. Take Victor Hugo, for example. He wrote amazing novels like Notre-Dame de Paris and Les Miserables, but he had to lock himself in his writing room without his fancy clothes to stop himself from going out and procrastinating.[16]

Then there's Douglas Adams, the guy behind The Hitchhiker's Guide to the Galaxy, which sold over 15 million copies! But get this: he was a total procrastinator and used to miss deadlines all the time. His editor even had to lock him in a hotel room with only food and drink until he finished his book![17]

Dr. Samuel Johnson was another famous procrastinator, and he wrote the first English language dictionary! But he would always leave his compositions to the last minute, and the only way he could finish his famous essay was by having an errand boy waiting outside his door to take it to the press.[18]

Even successful writers like Margaret Atwood struggle with procrastination. She's won awards like the Man Booker Prize, but she admits to spending her mornings procrastinating and worrying before finally diving into her work around 3:00.[19,20,21]

So, procrastination is no joke. It can hold us back, but these writers have shown us that we can overcome it with some tactics and techniques. It's all about finding what works for you and sticking to it. Now, enough procrastinating - let's get to work!

John - The Student

Hey, y'all! Let me tell you about John, the grad student who thought he could take his sweet time on his final project. John had a whole year to work on it, so he thought he could just wing it and turn it in at the last minute. Sound familiar?

John made a fancy chart called a Gant chart. It showed his project plan, but he quickly fell behind. He kept changing his deadlines, and before he knew it, he was in danger of getting kicked out of school. Yikes!

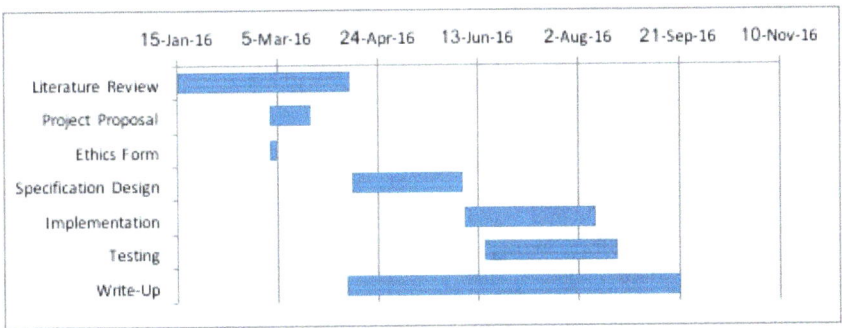

Big lesson: Fancy charts alone don't stop us from messing around.

But then, something miraculous happened. John finally got motivated and came up with a new plan. He worked like a madman, day, and night, until he finally finished his project. It wasn't perfect, but it was good enough.

The thing is, John had known all along that he needed to finish his project on time. But it wasn't until the consequences became real that he actually got off his butt and got to work. Why is that?

Well, it turns out that sometimes we need a little push to get us going. When the stakes are high and the consequences are real, we can tap into some serious motivation. And that's what happened with John.

But why do we keep doing this? Why do we keep sacrificing the quality of our work for silly distractions? Like scrolling through TikTok or playing video games for hours on end. And why do we only start working when there are serious consequences, like failing a class or missing a deadline?

Well, let's take John's story as an example. He was a grad student who kept putting off his final project until the last minute. But when the school threatened to kick him out, he suddenly found the motivation to get it done. Why does this happen to us too, even though we know we should be working hard all along?

It turns out, there's a lot going on in our brains that makes us procrastinate. But don't worry, we're not here to bore you with science. We just want to help you understand why you procrastinate and how to stop.

So, if you're like John and you tend to procrastinate until the last minute, don't beat yourself up. Just remember that sometimes all you need is a little kick in the pants to get going. And who knows? You might surprise yourself with what you can accomplish when you get motivated.

So, stay tuned, because we're going to break down the science of procrastination and give you some tips on how to be more productive. Trust me, you won't regret it!

Wendy - The Entrepreneur

Let me tell you another story. It's about Wendy - she's a total boss babe! Wendy's a CEO and founder of a consulting firm, where she basically helps other companies improve their processes and be better at what they do. Pretty cool, huh?

So, Wendy and her team have been working on this project for a whole month and they finally found a solution to a major corporation's challenge. They put together a super important document and passed it over to Wendy to turn into a killer pitch. No pressure or anything!

Wendy's got this, though. She's the team lead, after all. She breaks down the project into four parts and delegates each part to her colleagues, with the plan to pitch their idea in just three days. But then, things take a turn.

Wendy starts looking for PowerPoint templates on a website her friend recommended, and she gets sucked into a rabbit hole of articles about how to spend money wisely in a startup. Next thing she knows, it's seven hours later and she's only just finished reading all the articles.

The next day, Wendy's back on track and working hard on the PowerPoint presentation. But then she realizes that it depends on the report and the product design, so she spends another week going back and forth between the two.

Finally, Wendy's ready to present the project to her team and pick a date to approach the client. But then, one of her team members drops a bombshell - their competitor just made the exact same pitch to the same client and won the account!

It's all too clear now - Wendy was procrastinating on the parts of the project she didn't like or wasn't good at. We've all been there, right? But the lesson here is that sometimes, we got to push ourselves to do the hard stuff because it could make all the difference in the end.

So, keep hustling, and don't let procrastination hold you back!

Ben

Our next story is about a boy called Ben. He's the life of the party, always cracking jokes and keeping the vibes high. His crew loves hanging with him, saying he's the coolest dude around. But when it comes to relationships, Ben's track record isn't great. He's been in and out of them, and they all seem to end in disaster.

According to Ben, his exes thought he was too uptight and didn't have a sense of humor. But his boys don't buy it, they think he's funny as heck. So, after his last breakup, Ben decided to go to therapy to figure out what he was doing wrong. The counselor helped him figure out what he really wanted in a partner and to take things slow.

Eventually, Ben found his dream girl, and everything seemed perfect. They never argued, and he felt like they were on the same wavelength. But after eleven months, his friends noticed he was MIA from their hangouts. When they tried to check in, he was closed off. Something was up.

Ben realized that his girlfriend was becoming a bad influence on him. He was trying out new things and neglecting his friends. He knew he had to end things, but he kept putting it off. He even tried to avoid his girlfriend and her parents. But things only got worse, and he became more miserable.

So, what's going on with Ben? Well, it seems like he's stuck between his desire to be with his girlfriend and his need to take care of himself. He's afraid of hurting her, so he procrastinates on ending things. Plus, he's afraid of being alone and losing what he has with her.

But if he wants to move forward, he needs to overcome these fears. He can start by being honest with himself and acknowledging that the relationship isn't healthy for him. Then, he needs to have an honest conversation with his girlfriend about his feelings. It won't be easy, but it's necessary for his well-being.

Finally, he needs to lean on his friends for support. They care about him and want what's best for him. By opening up to them, he can get the encouragement he needs to take the next step.

In the end, Ben needs to remember that he deserves to be happy and healthy. It's okay to let go of something that isn't serving him. It may be tough, but he's got this!

Linda - The Employee

Meet Linda, she's a design staff at an electric car company and she's been working there for over seven years. But recently, her company went through some major changes. They laid off some older employees (including some of her pals), hired younger millennials, and redesigned the whole dang office. Now everyone's under crazy pressure to prove their worth, especially the older and more experienced staff like Linda.

One of their targets is to come up with a better car part design every year starting in January. But the deadline for submission is only announced 24 hours before, so it's a real race to the finish line. Linda decided to work on a new battery design on a Saturday in March because she knows everyone else is going to be working on a battery too. But then, she gets distracted by an email about her video streaming subscription. Linda's like, "Why am I still paying for this? I hardly ever watch anything on here." But then she sees the trailer for Infinity Wars and thinks it looks so cool. So, she decides to watch it on the giant wall screen in the common area. Just for two minutes, right?

Wrong. Linda ends up watching for an hour and only writes one page of the design spec. She keeps getting up to do dumb stuff like looking out the window and checking out her wig in the 360-degree mirror. Four months later, Linda still hasn't finished her design and she's making up excuses for herself. But here's the thing, missing the deadline could have serious consequences for her job and for her reputation. Plus, all her colleagues are submitting their designs every day, so she's falling behind big time.

But why isn't Linda motivated to work? And how can she get out of this funk? Well, as you read through this book, you'll learn all about it. Let's help Linda and ourselves get back on track and crush those goals, one day at a time!

Smith - The Professional

Let me tell you about Smith, the doctor who thought he had it all together. His colleagues worshiped him, and he was pretty confident in himself too. But deep down, he felt like he was meant for something else. So, he turned to meditation, self-development, and mentoring to figure it out.

Lo and behold, he realized he was super passionate about information technology! Smith wasn't about to let his busy schedule get in the way of pursuing his dream. He signed up for a bunch of self-taught programs and even enrolled in a tough master's program in computer engineering.

But then, one day at work, his colleagues were talking about this super addictive seasonal movie. They bet that if someone could watch the first two episodes without getting hooked, they'd do all their weekend shifts for two months. Smith didn't care about the bet, but when he got home, he thought he'd check out the trailer for the movie.

Well, he ended up watching not just the first two episodes, but the third, fourth, and fifth too! He was hooked and couldn't get enough. The suspense was killing him, and he just had to see what happened next.

But it wasn't all fun and games. Smith's binge-watching habit started to take over his life. He was staying up until 5am to watch episodes, missing his self-taught programs, and neglecting his studies. He even started using his mobile device to make class submissions instead of his laptop just so he could watch the movie during his commute.

It got so bad that he was procrastinating on everything just so he could watch more episodes. But finally, after [22] episodes, he kicked the habit. He realized it was taking a toll on his life and it wasn't worth it.

The same movie that once held him captive was now a distant memory. And guess what? Smith didn't even care about that stupid bet anymore. He was just glad to have his life back on track.

You

You definitely have your own experience. So, let's hear it. Write it down in the space below.

_____
_____
_____
_____
_____
_____
_____
_____
_____
_____
_____
_____
_____
_____
_____
_____
_____
_____
_____
_____
_____
_____
_____
_____
_____

So, we've all been there - you know, putting off important stuff until the last minute, or getting distracted by something totally irrelevant. But why do we do this? Is it just something we can't help? And how can we stop it from happening every darn time?

Well, fear not, my friends, because we're going to get to the bottom of this procrastination thing. We're going to look at all the research and information out there to figure out why we humans love to put things off. And we're not just talking hypothetical situations - we're going to look at real-life examples, like stuff that's happened to you, historical accounts, and even fictional characters.

And once we've got a handle on what's going on, we'll be able to create some tools to help you take control of your lives. So, let's get cracking and start learning how to kick procrastination to the curb!

PART 2
The Science Behind Messing Around

In this part, we're going to dive into all the juicy details. We'll talk about why messing around happens, what happens in your brain when you procrastinate, and how you can quit and get stuff done.
So, if you're ready to get stuff done and learn a thing or two about the science behind it, buckle up and get ready for a wild ride!

Chapter 3
Understanding Procrastination - Why We Do Everything Except What We Should

"What I don't understand about myself is that I decide one way, but then I act another, doing things I absolutely despise..."

Apostle Paul Romans 7: 15 (MSG Version)

I t is a bad thing. Procrastination is usually seen as a bad thing, but some people say it can be good too. Like when you're not sure what to do and need more time to figure it out. But don't be fooled, most of us agree that procrastination is not a cool thing to do. In this book, we'll only talk about the bad kind of procrastination.

Everyone knows what procrastination means, right? Well, not quite. People describe it in different ways, but they all agree on one thing: procrastination is when you put off doing something you were supposed to do. It's like, "I'll do it later," but you know you should do it now.22 That's procrastination, and we all do it, even though we know it's not the smartest move.

Sometimes it's okay to delay something that's not urgent, but when you procrastinate on something you need to do, that's when things get tricky. You're being irrational and not following through with your plans, even though you know it's not good for you. It's like you're working against yourself, and that's just not cool.

Knowing what procrastination is and how it works is the first step to beating it. But just knowing the definition won't solve the problem. You need to take action and stop procrastinating. It's not easy, but it's worth it. So, let's do this!

Biological vs Behavioral

So, procrastination is like that annoying friend who always shows up uninvited, overstays their welcome, and causes chaos in your life. But if we focus too much on why this friend keeps showing up, we might give up trying to get rid of them altogether. It's easy to blow the causes of procrastination out of proportion, but we can't deny that it has disastrous consequences.

Some folks think that procrastination is biological. Meaning that it is a type of medical condition, or that it is in our genes. These folks say it's because two parts of our brain are in a constant war with each other. One part, called the limbic system, is like the "pleasure center" and forms pleasurable opinions, causing addiction.[23,24] The other part, the prefrontal cortex, initiates, plans, and organizes.[25] People who believe that procrastination is biological, think that procrastinators have a less developed or dysfunctional prefrontal cortex that always gives in to the limbic system.

Just so you know. None of these two parts of the brain is the villain. They are both necessary for our survival. We need to differentiate and remember what events or activities were pleasurable so we can repeat them often. Plus, if we couldn't plan, organize, start tasks, and see them through, we'd still be living in the stone age.

Back to the scientists that think it's a biological issue. Even their most significant study couldn't say with certainty that those areas of the brain caused procrastination.[26] So, it's clear that their experiments helped us understand what these two different areas of our brains do; but failed to prove that biology is the root cause of procrastination.[27]

One thing we do know is that procrastination can be unlearned.[28] It's like the battle between a horse and its rider, with the horse seeking pleasure and avoiding discomfort and the rider trying to reason, plan, and execute. We face this battle every day, but we have the power to choose. And that's the key: we ultimately decide what's "more desirable" or "more comfortable." So, let's saddle up and rein in that metaphorical horse of procrastination!

Present Self vs Future Self

You know what's irrational? Procrastination. It's like when your friend John has a thesis due, but instead of working on it, he's playing video games or scrolling through TikTok. Not cool, John! And it's not just him - our pals Wendy, Ben, Linda, and Smith all did it too. They knew what they needed to do, but they still put it off in favor of other stuff.

But have you ever noticed that when you procrastinate, it's like someone else takes over? Like, there's the part of you that wants to get stuff done and achieve your goals, but then there's this other part that just wants to goof off and have fun. Researchers call these two parts the present-self and the future-self. The present-self is who you are right now, while the future-self is the version of you that you want to be in the future.

Here's the thing: the more connected you are with your future-self, the less likely you are to procrastinate.[29] That's because when you feel like your future-self is a part of you, you're more motivated to take action towards your goals. It's like, if you know you're going to be a successful author someday, you're more likely to sit down and write that essay for English class.

So, can we measure how connected we are to our future-self? That's a great question! If we can figure out how connected we are, we can work on increasing that connection and crushing our goals.

It is a Habit.

So, as humans, we're amazing creatures. We're adaptable, resourceful, and can basically handle anything that comes our way. But sometimes, we can get stuck in certain attitudes that limit us. These attitudes come from our traits, which are like hidden superpowers that shape our personalities. And while people can't see our traits, they can definitely see the characters or behaviors that we display because of them. So, if you're impulsive, people might see you as moody, even though they don't know the real reason behind your mood swings.[30]

Now, let's talk about procrastination. To really understand it, we need to talk about traits. Some people think there are three major traits, some say six, and others say there are sixteen! But for simplicity's sake, we'll stick with the "big" five: Conscientiousness, Agreeableness, Neuroticism, Openness to Experience, and Extraversion.[31] These traits have sub-traits, which in turn have facets or characters or behaviors that they manifest. And guess what? There's a relationship between traits and behavior! Basically, traits and habits are the key components of behavior.

We've got a handy table to show you what we mean!

TRAIT	SUB-TRAIT	CHARACTER
Neuroticism	Anxiety	Panic, Fear, Tense, Uneasiness
	Angry Hostility	Irritable
	Depression	Low self-esteem, not content, Chronic guilt, Self-directed anger
	Self-Consciousness	Shy, Paranoia
	Impulsive	Moody, Restlessness
	vulnerability	Lack of self-confidence
Extraversion	Activity	Energetic,
	Assertive	Forceful,
	Gregariousness	Sociable,
	Excitement-seeking	Adventurous,
	Positive Emotions	Enthusiastic
	Warmth	Outgoing, Friendly
Openness to Experience	Aesthetics	Artistic,
	Action	Varied interests,
	Fantasy	Imaginative,
	Feelings	Excitable,
	Ideas	Curious
	Values	Unconventional
Agreeableness	Altruism	Warm, Welcoming,
	Compliance	Not stubborn,
	Modesty	Not a show-off,
	Straightforwardness	Not demanding,
	Tender-mindedness	Sympathetic,
	Trust	Forgiving,
Conscientiousness	Achievement	Thorough, Hard working,
	Competence	Efficient,
	Deliberation	Not impulsive,
	Dutifulness	Not careless,
	Order	Organized
	Self-Discipline	Not Lazy

Check out the table up there! It's got the "big" five traits that all humans fall under - like, the foundational types we're grouped into. Your unique personality is created by a mix of these traits in different amounts, plus other stuff like culture and gender. And if you look closer, you'll see that there's a connection between traits and how we act. Basically, traits and habits are the big players when it comes to behavior.

So, what's the difference between a trait and a habit? Well, a trait is something you're born with, while a habit is something you learn over time. Traits are more biology-based, while habits are more nurture-based. Habits are things we do so often that we don't even think about them anymore, like brushing our teeth or scrolling through TikTok. And just like you can form a bad habit, you can also develop a good one by making the right choices.

So, is procrastination a trait or a habit? Drumroll please...it's a habit! Procrastination is something you learn to do over time, and it becomes so automatic that you don't even realize you're doing it. But here's the good news: you can break this habit. It's not something you're born with, it's something you cultivate. And just like any other habit, it can be broken with a little effort and awareness.

So, what makes us more likely to procrastinate? Well, according to research, certain traits are linked to procrastination. For example, people who are open to new experiences, extraverted, neurotic, and especially conscientious are more likely to procrastinate. That's because traits like conscientiousness have aspects like self-discipline and order that make it easier to get things done. On the other hand, traits like neuroticism can lead to impulsiveness and vulnerability, which make it harder to stick to a task.[32,33.]

The bottom line? Procrastination is a habit, not a trait. And just like any other habit, it can be broken with a little awareness and effort. So, next time you're tempted to put off that essay or clean your room, remember that you have the power to make a different choice. And who knows? Maybe one day you'll be known as the most productive person in the room!

Killer Habit

So, procrastination is not just a common habit, it's a killer habit. And no, we're not exaggerating. You see, putting off important actions that lead to success and fulfillment may seem harmless at first, but it can be super damaging.

Think about it: Waiting till the last minute to call a taxi for an interview can lead to arriving late, getting disoriented, and totally flopping the interview. Or, waiting till the last minute to prepare for a meeting could mean you show up unprepared, which is definitely not a good look. And don't even get us started on waiting too long to book a dinner reservation for a first date. Yikes!

But it's not just these little everyday things that can be affected.

Procrastination can lead to stunted academics, unfulfilled lives, shame, self-doubt, diminished health, and even death. Yeah, you heard that right - death. We're not kidding.

And the worst part? Procrastination actually makes you feel good, at least until it's too late. So, you keep putting things off, thinking you'll have more time later, but that's not always the case.

There have been studies that prove this too. One study showed that students who turned in their papers late got a lower score and experienced more stress and physical symptoms as the deadline approached.[34] So, if you keep procrastinating, you're not only setting yourself up for failure, but you're also putting your health and well-being at risk.

So, the next time you feel the urge to put something off, just remember that procrastination is a killer habit. Don't let it take over your life and lead you down a path of regret.

Quotes

Listen up. Here's a tip - sometimes it's better to learn from the mistakes of others rather than making your own. And who better to learn from than those who have made great achievements in life? If they could do it, then we can too! So, let's take a look at some epic quotes that will help us win the battle against procrastination.

First up, we have the wise words of Benjamin Franklin: "You may delay, but time will not, and lost time is never found again." So, don't wait around because time is not going to wait for you.

Abraham Lincoln also chimes in with, "Things may come to those who wait, but only the things left by those who hustle." That's right, waiting around for things to happen won't get you anywhere. You need to get out there and hustle!

Thomas Jefferson reminds us that, "Never put off for tomorrow what you can do today." Don't be lazy, get stuff done today!

Norman Vincent Pearl shares the secret to happiness, "The really happy people are those who have broken the chains of procrastination, those who find satisfaction in doing the job at hand. They're full of eagerness, zest, productivity. You can be too." So, break free from the chains of procrastination and be productive!

Karen Lamb gives us a glimpse into the future with, "A year from now, you may wish you had started today." Don't regret not starting earlier, start now!

Finally, Charles Swindoll and Napoleon Hill give us a double dose of inspiration. Swindoll says, "The habit of always putting off an experience until you can afford it, or until the time is right, or until you know how to do, it is one of the greatest burglars of joy. Be deliberate, but once you've made up your mind, jump in." And Hill reminds us, "Don't wait, the time will never be just right."

So, there you have it, folks! Some epic quotes to motivate you to stop procrastinating and start achieving your goals. Let's break free from the chains of laziness and be productive!

Why We Prefer Messing Around till the Last Minute

We've all heard that we should keep our eyes on the prize and avoid goofing around. It's basic knowledge that procrastination can be a bad look. But even with all that good advice, we still end up procrastinating. So, what gives? Why can't we just get it together and do what needs to be done? Well, it turns out that the answer to that question is different depending on who you ask. Procrastinators will give you a sob story or try to justify their actions. Meanwhile, non-procrastinators will be like, "Bruh, you're just being lazy."

Alright, check it out guys. When we try to tackle procrastination, we can basically break down the reasons why we do it into two categories.

First, there's a group of people who don't really understand what procrastination is all about. They think it's just a fancy way of saying "being lazy" or something like that. And let's be real, we've all been there before, and messing around or procrastination is not just because you are lazy.

Then there's the other group who actually knows what procrastination is, but they're just using the wrong methods to deal with it. Like trying to force themselves to work for hours on end without taking any breaks, or just hoping that their motivation will magically appear out of thin air.

Luckily, we are going to be creating tools that will solve the problem of procrastinating for both groups. So, just know that all you need is a bit of effort and the right approach, you can definitely overcome procrastination and start getting stuff done!

.

Chapter 4
How Procrastination Works - The Engine Room of F... ing Around

"I wasted time, and now doth time waste me."
—William Shakespeare

Dissected. Alrighty, let's dive into the nitty-gritty of procrastination! We need to get down and dirty to figure out how this beast works. The more we learn, the better equipped we'll be to kick its butt and get stuff done.

So, to start off, we're going to look at some stories, examples, and your own experiences to find some commonalities. It may seem like these people have nothing in common - John's a student, Wendy's a business owner, Ben lives with his mom - but they all have one thing in common: they procrastinate!

Even the most disciplined people can fall victim to procrastination, like Colonel John Rall and General McClellan. These guys were professional soldiers who grew up with strict rules and a zero-tolerance policy for delay, yet they still couldn't get their acts together when it really counted.

So, what's the deal? Well, it turns out that while we may want something, we may not want to do the work required to get it. Doesn't that sound familiar? For example, John wants to pass his project class, but he doesn't necessarily want to write the paper that's required to pass. Wendy wants to win the client, but she doesn't necessarily want to draft a preliminary product design or write an executive summary.

And then there's the competition for our attention - all the other things we could be doing instead of the task at hand. Maybe Ben would rather hang out with his friends than deal with his relationship issues, or Smith would rather watch a movie than work on a project for work.

But fear not, my procrastinating friend! We are moving forward already, and we've already identified some commonalities among procrastinators.
1. First, there's what we really want to achieve - the end goal. Then,
2. There's the task we need to complete to achieve that goal - the action. And finally,
3. There's the other stuff we do instead of the task at hand - the inaction.

So, whenever you procrastinate, there are three things that are present, which you must identify. So, take a good hard look at your own procrastination habits. And identify the following:

1. What is the end goal you're trying to achieve?
2. What task do you need to complete to get there? And,
3. What other stuff are you doing instead of that task?

Write it all down and see if you can identify any patterns. Once you know what's holding you back, you'll be one step closer to kicking procrastination's butt!

S/No.	**End Goal**	**Action**	**Inaction**
	What I want to achieve	What I need to do to achieve it	That other thing I am doing that I shouldn't
1			
2			
3			

Checkout the example below for our friends, John, Wendy, Ben Linda, and Smith.

Actor	End Goal	Action	Inaction
John	Pass the project class	Write thesis	Anything but writing thesis
Wendy	Win the client	1. Create PowerPoint presentation. 2. Synthesize report from her team.	1. Internet surfing. 2. Worry over startup.
Ben	Breakup with Helen	1. Talk with Helen	1. Engaging in aspects of relationship he enjoys. 2. Change Helen to suit him.
Linda	Be seen as very relevant	1. Create new battery design	1. Internet surfing. 2. Movie bingeing 3. Anything but creating design.
Smith	Have the benefits of not watching it	1. Keep established routine	1. Movie bingeing
You			

Hey teens, let's take another look at the examples in the table above. They all have one thing in common - the actors, another general name for our friends - keep switching between action and inaction. John goes back and forth between writing his thesis and doing anything else he can think of. Wendy jumps between creating a PowerPoint presentation and surfing the web. Linda can't decide if she wants to design a new battery or just binge-watch movies and stress about her hair. And don't even get me started on Ben and his avoidance tactics with Helen.

But here's the kicker - this pattern of switching between action and inaction is what makes procrastination so darn frustrating! It's like we want to get stuff done, but we can't seem to stick to it. So, let's break it down. Whenever we procrastinate, there are four key elements at play: the end goal or result we want, the action we need to take, the inaction we switch to, and the act of switching itself.

To really beat procrastination, we need to figure out what's going on with that switch. Why do we keep flipping it on and off? And what can we do to keep it in the "on" position more often? Stay tuned, because in the next sections, we'll dive deeper into the world of action and inaction. We'll explore what makes that switch flip, and how we can take control of it.

Action Vs Inaction

Hey there, friends! Let's talk about taking action (or not taking action, if you're like the former me). It turns out that every time we put things off, it's because we have the wrong idea about what it means to take action. We switch back and forth between actually doing something and just sitting around because of this misunderstanding. So, we need to figure this out, my friends.

First of all, let's look at how we think about action and inaction when we're procrastinating. We know what we need to do, but we're not doing it. Instead, we're doing other things that we consider more enjoyable or important. These "alternate tasks" are the things we do instead of working on the real task at hand.

But as time goes on and the deadline approaches, we start to see these alternate tasks as a waste of time. They're not helping us get any closer to finishing the actual task, so they become less appealing. This change in perspective helps us to stop procrastinating and start taking action on the real task.

The problem is that we've been trained to think that inaction is just doing nothing, and that it's a neutral state that doesn't affect our work. But that's not true! Inaction is actually doing something else instead of the task we're supposed to be working on. So, we need to redefine action and inaction in terms of our goals.

We need to ask ourselves: is this the activity that I should be doing right now to move forward with my project? If the answer is no, then it's inaction, even if it seems important or valuable. We need to identify these alternate tasks that we use to procrastinate and see them as the distractions from the original task, so we can stay focused and avoid distractions.

Sometimes it's hard to know what action and inaction are, especially when there are multiple paths to take. But by understanding the negative consequences of inaction, we can start to identify those activities that are actually holding us back from achieving our goals. So, let's take a closer look at our own procrastination stories and see what alternate tasks we've been using to procrastinate. Use the form below to write them down.

Write down a list of alternate tasks that you've used to procrastinate. Think deeply!

1._____
2._____
3._____
4._____
5._____
6._____
7._____
8._____
9._____
10._____

The Switch

So, we've figured out that when it comes to procrastination, we've got two choices - doing the thing we're supposed to be doing or doing something else instead (which we like to call "inaction"). And from watching ourselves and others procrastinate, we know that we tend to switch back and forth between these two choices. Basically, we only get back to work when we're forced to, by a deadline or something like that.

We can see this in all our examples - like John, who can't focus on his thesis and ends up doing everything else under the sun until the deadline is staring him in the face. Or Wendy, who's supposed to be working on specific tasks but gets sidetracked by playing with PowerPoint and scrolling through the internet. Even Ben, who's supposed to be breaking up with his girlfriend, ends up trying to change her behavior instead of just getting it over with. Linda's supposed to be designing a battery, but instead she's watching movies and answering emails. And let's not forget Smith, who should be studying online but can't resist the temptation of a good old seasonal movie.

So, the question is - why do we do this? What makes us switch from action to inaction, and vice versa? And how can we understand this phenomenon better? Well, stick around, because in this chapter we're going to dive deep into the mysteries of procrastination and figure out what's really going on here.

Desirableness

So, on a regular day, we all have a bunch of stuff to do. Some things are planned, while others just come up randomly. We must decide which ones we want to do, which ones we want to put off, and which ones we want to scrap altogether. And let's be real, we usually go for the things that seem most appealing, while avoiding the ones that seem like a drag. Research has shown that this is just human nature—we're wired to seek out the good stuff and avoid the bad.[35]

But there's more to it than that. See, it's not just a matter of whether something is good or bad. It's also about how good or bad it is. Take a procrastinator, for example. They might have to write a boring thesis, but instead they'll write some fun poems. Sure, both involve writing, but one definitely feels less terrible.

And when we look at our stories, we see just how much our preferences can influence our procrastination. John put off his thesis until the last possible moment, but as the deadline got closer, suddenly the thesis seemed a lot more appealing than all those other distractions. Wendy loves playing with PowerPoint designs, so when given four tasks to choose from, she goes for the one she likes best. And even when presented with a more appealing option, she ditches her work to surf the web instead.

33

Ben doesn't have an easy choice like that. He's stuck between two equally undesirable options: staying in a relationship he's not happy with or ending it and looking like a failure. So, he puts it off, even though it's causing him grief. Linda's got a bunch of work to do, but she keeps getting sidetracked by more enjoyable activities, like watching movies or checking her email. And Smith was doing just fine until he is introduced to a new episode of a popular show, which was way more appealing than his boring coursework.

Take a minute to think about a time when you procrastinated. Chances are that the thing you switched to was more appealing than what you were supposed to be doing. It's just how our brains work. And that's why procrastination is such a tricky thing to overcome.

Triggers

Okay, so let's talk about why we do what we do (or don't do what we're supposed to do). Basically, whether we decide to take action or sit on our butts depends on how desirable or undesirable the options are. But hold up, it's not just as simple as "good" or "bad." There are actually a ton of things that can influence how desirable something is. Check out the picture below to get an idea.

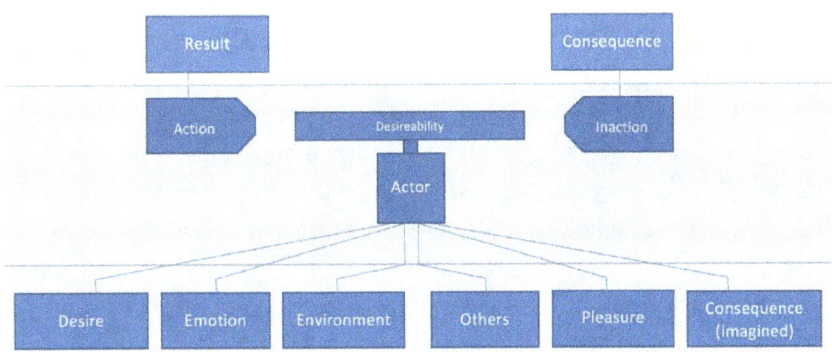

Have you checked it out? The fancy picture above shows how procrastination works, and most importantly, how to overcome it. So, pay attention, okay?

First things first, if you want to get results, you've got to take action. But if you choose to do nothing instead, be ready to face the music (or the consequences, if you want to be formal about it).

Now, here's the deal: what determines whether you take action or not is something called desirability. It's like a switch that can either connect you to the path of action or disconnect you and send you down the road of inaction.

And guess what? A bunch of factors influence that switch, such as your desires, emotions, environment, what brings you pleasure, and who or what influences you. Plus, there are other custom factors that can vary from person to person.

So, we will take out time to explain all these factors, which are desire, emotion, environment, consequence, pleasure, passion, and others.

1. Desire:

Humans are a curious bunch, always looking for the next new thing to try out. You're no different, and you also like to be in control of your surroundings. And I am sure you've noticed that it seems like your desires are never-ending, because once you get what you want, you're already onto the next thing. You might think that as long as you get what you want in the end, everything will be smooth sailing, but that's not always the case. As much as you're wired to want things, you also want to get them without putting in too much effort. That's why sometimes you end up daydreaming about what you want instead of taking action. It's just easier that way, even though it's not necessarily the most effective. But to achieve your goals, you need to understand your desires and learn how to use them to your advantage.

So, what is desire, exactly? Well, it's when you really want something that doesn't exist yet or isn't in the form that you want it to be. This makes you want to take action to make it happen. However, not all desires are created equal - some are stronger than others and make you more likely to take action. For example, a wish is a pretty weak desire that doesn't usually lead to action. A drive, on the other hand, is a much stronger desire that's often biological in nature. An impulse is a sudden desire that makes you act without thinking too much, while a compulsion is an even stronger impulse that's hard to resist. Longing and craving are also strong desires, but they're focused on things that are currently out of reach.[36]

So, why does all this matter? Well, it matters because desires can be powerful motivators for action - but not always. Sometimes, even if you really want something, you still won't take action to get it. So, it's important to understand how desire works and how it affects your motivation to take action.[37] We know that desire is what inspires action, but like we said, not all desires are created equal.[38] The strength and consistency of your desire can determine how much you're willing to do to make it happen.

To overcome procrastination, we need to answer some important questions about desire. Where does it come from? Can we control it? And does having a stronger desire for something automatically make us more likely to take action to make it happen? By understanding the answers to these questions, we can learn how to use our desires to motivate us to achieve our goals.

How Desires Are Formed: Hey there! So, have you heard of the latest tech releases lately? If you have, then you must have heard a thing or two about those Apps that seem so addictive. Do you know that those Apps that you love so much, are actually desire creating Apps? That is gist for another day. But let's talk about how desires are formed. Desires, they are that feeling you get when you really want something, whether it's a material object or something intangible like status or recognition. We all have desires, and they come from a place of lacking something. Sometimes it's because of our basic needs, like food or water, but other times it's because we want something that we see others have. That's where observation comes in - we see other people with something and think, "Hey, I want that too!" It's like when you see someone with a new phone and suddenly your old one seems outdated. But it's not just about what we see - we also make analogical inferences based on what we observe. For example, if Paul, Peter, and James all have cars, and I'm like them, then I can have a car too, right? That's how we form desires - by observing and making connections. But even when we're not consciously aware of it, that process is still happening. So, what's something you've been wanting lately?

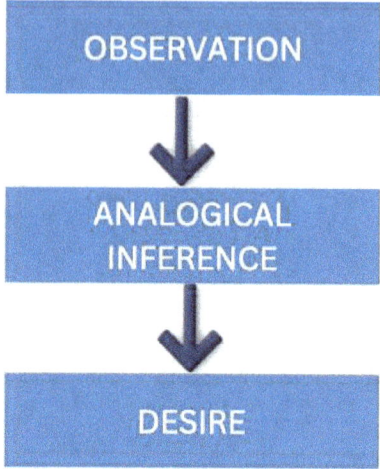

It also turns out, that there are a bunch of things that can cause desire to pop up. One of those things is emotions. And get this, once you're feeling all desire-y, it can actually feed back into your emotions! So, basically, desire and emotions are like two peas in a pod. They're tight like that.[39]

Desire Instigates Action: So, we've been talking about desires and how they come to be in our minds. And here's the thing, all desires should lead to action, but sometimes they don't. It all depends on how intense the desire is. The stronger the desire, the more likely we are to take action and get stuff done. But we have to be conscious about regulating and controlling our desires, not just suppressing them. Because suppressing desires? That just backfires.[40]

To regulate and control our desires, we must measure their intensity. And there are two things to look at: how much they make us want to take action, and how much they grab our attention. Once we've figured that out, we can use some "desire tools" to make sure we're taking action and not procrastinating.

But here's the tricky part: just because we really, really want something

37

doesn't mean we are going to be all committed to getting it. Sometimes we get too focused on the end result and forget about the journey. And that's when we fall into the trap of procrastination.

So, bottom line? We have to use our desires to motivate us and move us forward. But we can't forget about the process along the way. In the next chapter, we'll talk about some ways to make sure we're staying on track and not letting procrastination get in the way.

2. Emotion

Guys and gals! We all know that emotions are a part of our lives, whether we're fighting in a war zone or just chilling at home with our parents. Emotions are like a sneaky little ninja that creeps up on us when we least expect it. They can be triggered by anything - people, events, situations, activities, objects, or even the environment. And when they do hit us, we react. Sometimes we react like superheroes, and other times we react like scaredy-cats. It all depends on the situation.

Now, let's talk about how our emotions can affect our decision making and lead us down the path of procrastination. When we're faced with a task we don't really like, negative emotions like fear and anger can rear their ugly heads and make us feel overwhelmed, ashamed, or worried. We just want to get away from these emotions, so we shift our focus to short-term fixes, like watching a movie or scrolling through social media. This distraction causes us to procrastinate and put off the task at hand.

But wait, there's more! Our emotions can also be attached to certain tasks, whether positive or negative. For example, Wendy might have a positive emotional attachment to her startup, which causes her to procrastinate on other tasks in favor of working on her business. On the other hand, Ben might have a negative emotional attachment to breaking up with someone, which causes him to procrastinate on that task.

So, what can we do about it? Well, the first step is to be aware of how our emotions are affecting us. Once we know that, we can start to take control of our decision-making and avoid procrastination. We can also try to create positive emotions and attach them to the tasks we don't like or find ways to make those tasks trigger positive emotions. That way, we'll be more motivated to tackle them head-on.

So, how do you think your emotions affect your decision making? What tasks do you procrastinate on and why? Take a moment to ponder these questions and see if you can come up with some answers. And don't forget to use the form below to personalize your answers!

Trigger	Emotion Triggered	Feeling
Activity or situation that triggers an emotion	Emotion that is triggered when you engage in the activity listed	What you feel when the emotion is triggered

How Emotions Are Formed: So, you now know a few things that triggers an emotion in you. Let's now talk about how they're created. So, there are a few different ideas floating around about this. Some people think emotions are a state - like you're just in a happy or sad mood, you know? Others think it's more of a process. And if it's a process, there's a debate about whether it's a "cognitive" process or a "noncognitive" process.

Okay, okay, I know those are some pretty big words. Basically, if it's a cognitive process, that means your brain is doing some fancy data manipulation to create your emotions. But if it's noncognitive, it's more like your emotions are just a knee-jerk reaction to things happening around you.

But let's get real with Mary and Ann, two strangers who meet at an airport gate and end up sitting next to each other on an 11-hour flight.
Imagine the following scenarios:

- Scenario 1: On the flight and Mary is chowing down on her meal when suddenly, Ann her seatmate spills water all over her. Ugh, talk about a wet t-shirt contest. But luckily, Ann apologizes like crazy, and they both move on from it. Phew, crisis averted!

- Scenario 2: Alright, so the super long flight continues, and Ann is finally able to catch some Z's. But then, she starts snoring and Mary her seatmate is NOT having it. She knows this because Mary keeps waking her up and it's annoying AF. And then, to make matters worse, while Ann is half awake, she notices that Mary straight up pours water on her! Not cool, dude. She wakes up fully, to a halfhearted apology from Mary, with a smirk on her face. What a way to ruin your beauty sleep!

- Scenario 3: Alright, let's switch it up a bit. Imagine a repeat of scenario 1, but this time, Ann is blind, and Mary accidentally spills water on Ann Just like in the first scenario.

- Scenario 4: Again, imagine a repeat of scenario 2, with Ann blind this time.

In scenarios 1 and 2, two different types of emotions will be triggered in Ann. Ann will probably smile at Mary in the first scenario and be livid in the second. In these two examples, we can see that emotions happen automatically without us even really thinking about it. But in scenarios 3 and 4, where Mary is blind, we see that our brains does process some information and make judgments even if we're not consciously aware of it.

Can you see why that is? Okay let's spill it. In scenario 3, Ann will also not take offense. But in scenario 4, we will all agree that even though Ann is blind and unable to see the smirks; she will take offense. This is because Ann, is just like everyone of us. She also relies on her sensory organs - eyes, ears, nose, and skin- to take in information from the world around us in everyday situations. And so, Ann's brain would have noticed and stored the information that Mary does not like her sleeping and snoring. Ann's brain would have also stored the tone of Mary's voice when she apologized genuinely the first time. So, when Mary apologizes this second time, Ann's brain will automatically remember "Mary doesn't like me sleeping". Ann's brain will also remember that Mary's tone of voice and choice of words is definitely different this time. This will lead to an anger emotion being triggered in Ann.

So, basically, our eyes, ears, nose, and skin take in information from the world around us, and our brains compare that information to past experiences. If the information matches up with something that previously made us happy, mad, sad, or whatever, then we automatically feel that emotion again. It's like we have a little library of emotions in our heads that keeps getting updated every time we experience something new.

So, there you have it, folks. Emotions are a process, and our brains are doing some serious behind-the-scenes work to make it happen. And if you're like me, your library of emotions probably looks a little something like Ann's table below.

Scenario	Data	Information	Emotion Elicited
Scenario 1	Look in eyes. Shaped mouth	Contrition	Happy
Scenario 2	Look in eyes. Shaped mouth	Smirk	Anger
Scenario 3	Words spoken. Tone of voice	Contrition	Happy
Scenario 4	Words spoken. Tone of voice	Smirk	Anger

Okay, so get this - turns out that whole "non-cognitive" thing when it comes to emotion formation is just a big fat illusion. Yeah, it might seem like our feelings just pop up out of nowhere, but that's only because the process happens so darn fast!

Now, we're on board with the cognitive theorists who say that there's actually a lot of thinking going on behind the scenes. Here's how it works: first, we encounter something that triggers an emotional response (could be anything from a cute puppy to a scary movie). Then, we start evaluating that trigger - is it good or bad, safe, or dangerous? Finally, based on that evaluation, we form our emotion. It's like a little emotional assembly line!

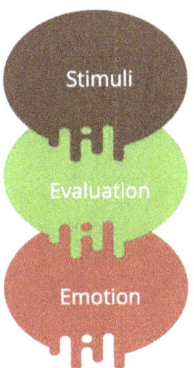

Emotion Instigates Action: So, you know how people often think that rational thinking and emotions are like two opposite sides of the spectrum? Well, let me tell you, it's not as black and white as that.

Emotions aren't always the result of careful thinking, but that doesn't mean they're completely irrational. In fact, emotions are patterns that develop over time as you grow up. They help you figure out if something is good or bad for you, and if you should take action.

You might have noticed that in many cases, your gut feeling provides a more accurate assessment of a situation than your rational thinking. And that's because emotions are directly linked to your actions, even if you don't realize it.

So, the next time someone tells you to "use your head, not your heart," just remember that emotions are an important part of our decision-making process.

Emotion and Decision Making: Alright, check this out guys! We all know that our emotions have a HUGE impact on the decisions we make every day. And it's not just me saying it — there's actual scientific proof! Studies show that patients who have damage to the part of their brain that processes emotions are unable to make rational decisions.[41] Crazy, right?

So, when emotions are triggered in our brain, our nervous system responds by creating physical sensations in our body. These sensations then help guide our responses — whether we take action or do nothing. It's a pretty cool process, and you can see how it all works in the diagram below:

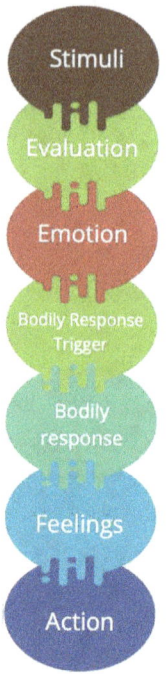

So, emotions are a tricky thing, and they affect the decisions we make.[42] Yep, it's true! Sometimes emotions can be so subtle that we don't even notice the bodily response. But that doesn't mean they're not affecting us.

We've all been there - feeling surprised, shocked, or just plain old astonished. Haven't you? I bet you have. I am sure that you've noticed that when we feel surprised, for example, it can cause a bunch of different feelings like eagerness, astonishment, and shock. And each of these feelings can lead to different actions. Eagerness might make you go for it, astonishment might leave you frozen, and shock might send you running in the other direction.

Look at the emotion wheel - it's like a colorful pie chart of all the different emotions and feelings we can have. So, if you want to become more aware of the type of decisions you make when faced with emotions, take a closer look at the emotion wheel.

colored version courtesy of Photo via Instagram / @trainingsbyromy

Have you taken a good look at the emotion wheel? Which feelings make you procrastinate? It's worth taking the time to figure it out. Trust me, you'll thank yourself later.

If you've done that, to make things easy peasy lemon squeezy, let's create a handy-dandy table. That way, we can keep track of everything and refer to it later. Sound good? Great! Let's get to it!

Feelings	Decision

Below is an example:

Feelings	Decision
Eagerness	Engage task at hand
Overwhelmed	Abandon task, rationalize postponement
Awe	Less aggressive and open further engagement
Fulfilled	Confidently take on more tasks

Emotion and Procrastination: Alrighty, so we've learned that emotions play a big role in our decision-making process, and that we can actually influence how we react to them by being aware of what triggers them. And while it's easy to take action when we're feeling good, it's not always that simple. Sometimes, certain tasks can trigger negative emotions that make us want to run in the opposite direction. That's where procrastination comes in![43]

So, let's do a little exercise. Think of some tasks that give you good vibes and some that give you bad vibes. Maybe playing video games gives you a rush of excitement, while doing your math homework makes you want to curl up and cry. Now, let's talk about how those emotions can lead to procrastination.

If a task makes you feel good, like playing video games, it's easy to get swept up in the fun and forget about everything else. But when it comes to less enjoyable tasks, like homework, negative emotions can take over and make it hard to focus. It's like our brains are wired to avoid anything that could cause discomfort or pain, even if it means putting off something important.

So, what can we do about it? Well, first we need to be aware of what's going on. Recognizing when negative emotions are taking over can help us stop procrastination in its tracks. Then, we can start using some of the emotional tools we'll talk about later to help us push through and get things done. But for now, just think about those tasks and how they make you feel. It's a good first step towards understanding why we procrastinate.

So many emotions and feelings have a sleezy connection with procrastination. Such that we cannot talk about all of them one after the other. But let's take a look at some of them.

Guilt:

So, guilt is a feeling that pops up when you do something you know is wrong. It's like your conscience is telling you "Hey, that was not cool, dude". The good thing about guilt is that it can motivate you to make things right. But if you keep doing the same wrong thing over and over again, guilt can turn into a big bully that makes you feel helpless and defeated.

Here's the tricky part: when you feel guilty, you can either try to fix things or come up with excuses to justify your actions. If you choose to fix things, then guilt is a good thing because it can help you get stuff done. But if you make excuses and rationalize your behavior, then guilt becomes a big roadblock to productivity. And that's when procrastination shows up like "Hey, let's not deal with this guilt thing right now. Let's watch some cat videos instead!"

So, to sum it up: guilt can cause procrastination or be caused by procrastination. It all depends on how you deal with it. Don't let guilt boss you around, but don't ignore it either. Listen to your conscience, take responsibility for your actions, and try to make things right.

Shame:

When you mess up and feel like you've done something wrong, the feeling of shame pops up like a Jack-in-the-box. This emotion makes you want to run, hide, or deny what you did. And when you're the type of person who always wants things to be perfect, shame can be a real killer of productivity.

Perfectionists are scared of failure, so they tend to avoid tasks that they think they can't complete to their own high standards. They're so afraid of feeling ashamed if they mess up that they'll put things off until the cows come home. This means that the feeling of shame can be a real enabler of procrastination, especially when combined with perfectionism.[44] So, if you're always feeling like you're not good enough, it might be time to look into why you're holding yourself to such high standards.

Anxiety:

Anxiety is basically when your brain goes into "potential danger" mode, and makes you feel worried or scared. But here's the thing - anxiety can actually be helpful sometimes! It can motivate you to take action and deal with whatever's causing the anxiety. On the other hand, it can also make you feel overwhelmed and just...worry. So, it's kind of a double-edged sword.

Fear:
Fear is not just that feeling you get when you see a spider crawling on your wall. Nope, fear can also be the reason why you're procrastinating on that big project or presentation. It's triggered by anything that's perceived as a threat to your well-being or success. And when fear sets in, your body responds with sweating, increased heart rate, and adrenaline pumping through your veins. But the most important thing to note is that fear can lead to the fight-or-flight response, which means you either face the fear head-on or run away from it.

When it comes to procrastination, there are a bunch of fears that can hold you back. These include fear of the unknown, fear of change, fear of failure, fear of rejection, fear of disapproval, and more. But fear of failure is the big kahuna. It's that feeling you get when you think you're going to mess up and disappoint everyone. And that fear can stop you dead in your tracks, preventing you from taking any action at all.

But fear isn't the only emotion that can lead to procrastination. Shame, guilt, anxiety, and other feelings can also be culprits. The important thing is to recognize how these emotions are affecting you and find ways to overcome them. So, take a look at the wheel of emotions and see which ones are holding you back. Once you've identified them, you'll be one step closer to beating procrastination and achieving your goals.

3. Environment

Your surroundings play a big part in your life. That's why people always say that after genetics, the environment you live in has a big impact on who you are. Every job or task you do happens within an environment. Sometimes, it's inside a building, and other times it's outside. Your environment can be broken down into two main categories: natural and man-made. The natural part includes things that are outside your control, like the weather. But the man-made part is created by humans, which means we have the power to change it. And this man-made part includes things like the color of the room, the temperature, where we school, or work, and so on. Believe it or not, all these components can influence how productive you are and whether you procrastinate or not.[45] So, the question is, can we use our environment to make tasks more appealing and switch off our procrastination? Let's take a closer look at these environmental components and find out.

Color:

Did you know that colors can have a huge impact on your life? Like seriously, it's been proven that the color of the plate you eat on can even affect how your dessert tastes![46] But it doesn't stop there, colors can also impact your mood, productivity, and perception.[47] And get this, it's not just some random thing that's different for each person, research has shown that our reactions to colors can be accurately predicted!

So which colors have what effects? Well, blue is great for offices because it's intellectual and inspires trust and logical thinking. Red is more physical and can be used in areas where there's a lot of physical activity because it inspires excitement, strength, and courage. But be careful, too much red can mess with your logical reasoning. Green, on the other hand, is associated with balance, creative thinking, and nature. It's perfect for home offices or places where you need to work for long hours because it's easy on the eyes.

Yellow and purple, though, are a bit more stimulating, so use them sparingly. Remember, the intensity and brightness of a color matter too. Low saturation or intensity is calming and relaxing, while high saturation or intensity is energizing and stimulating.[48] So, if you want to switch up your environment to get more productive and kick procrastination to the curb, think about what colors you're surrounded by and how they're making you feel.[49]

Workspace:

Okay, let's give this a shot: Let's talk about workspace productivity. First off, workspace is not only for people who have paid jobs. Workspace also includes where you study, do your homework or do deep thinking. So, you know the drill - tidy up that mess, get yourself an ergonomic chair and desk, yada yada yada. But did you know that some things in your workspace could be tempting you to procrastinate? That's right, your environment can be your own worst enemy! So, it's time to get real and make some changes. Don't just settle for what's around you - find what works best for you and kick those procrastination-inducing items to the curb. Because when it comes to your workspace, it's not just about chairs and desks. Let's get to the nitty-gritty of what's really affecting your productivity.

Location:
Picture this: you're at Disney World with your family, trying to finish a project for school. Or you're working in an all-glass office in the middle of a shopping mall in Dubai - looks like a future thingy. How much work do you think you'll get done? Let's compare that to working alone on an island resort. Obviously, the chances of getting work done in the third scenario are way higher than the first two. Now, we can't all jet off to an island resort every time we need to get work done, and not all work can be done remotely. But this goes to show that where you work matters. Some students may find the library to be their productivity palace, while others prefer the hustle and bustle of a classroom. And some may even retreat to a quiet corner of the school stadium. Long story short, our environment has the power to flip the switch between action and inaction.

4. Pleasurableness

Hey there! So, did you know that humans are basically pleasure-seeking beings? Yup, we spend our whole lives either trying to avoid pain or trying to get that sweet, sweet pleasure fix. And the things that bring us pleasure are usually external — like stuff, events, or activities. The only bummer is that when those things go away, the pleasure goes with them too.

But here's the real kicker — the more pleasure you get from doing something, the more you're going to want to keep doing it. That's just how our brains work! We're wired to seek out pleasure and to keep seeking it out until we're totally hooked. This is what scientists call "hedonic adaptation" and it's actually pretty cool. It's helped us humans to adapt to all sorts of changes over time, like when the weather gets hotter or there's not enough food around.

But here's the downside — if something's not super pleasurable, we're probably not going to want to do it. And if there's something else, we could be doing that's way more pleasurable, we're probably going to put off doing the less-fun thing until the last possible moment. That's why procrastination is such a huge problem for so many people.

So, how do we fix it? Well, we must figure out what makes us feel pleasure in the first place. The thing is pleasure is totally subjective. What feels good to one person might not feel good to another. Like, imagine three people win the lottery and they all get a painting by Pablo Picasso as their prize. One person might love it, one person might be meh about it, and one person might straight-up hate it. It's all about personal preference.

And there are all sorts of things that can influence our perceptions of pleasure. Like, our past experiences can make us associate certain things with good feelings or bad feelings. Or our culture might tell us that certain things are "good" or "bad."[50,51] It's all kind of a mess, really.

But here's the good news — if we can figure out how to make the stuff, we need to do more pleasurable, we might stop procrastinating so much. So, let's get to it!

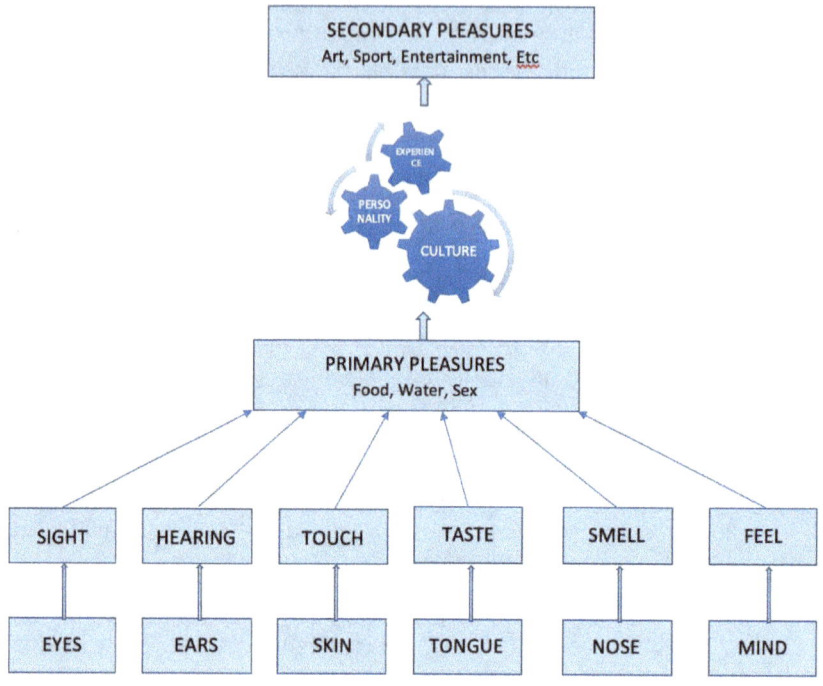

Hey, so now that we know what's up with pleasure, it's time to apply it to the dreaded P-word: procrastination. But hold up, fam, here's the big question: if we make one activity way more pleasurable than another, does that automatically make it more appealing? Like, are we going to be all over the activity that brings us the most joy, even if it's not the most important thing on our to-do list?

Well, after some real talk, we can say that yeah, we're more likely to choose the activity that brings us more pleasure. So now we got to ask ourselves: how can we use this knowledge to our advantage? And can we change the pleasure we get from certain activities to stop ourselves from procrastinating? These are the real questions, peeps.

5. Consequence (Imagined)

Consequences - yeah, they are those things we always try to avoid but can't escape. It's like that one annoying classmate who's always trailing behind you. Whenever you take an action, whether big or small, you can bet your bottom dollar that a consequence will come knocking.

In this book, we're talking about unpleasant consequences, the ones that make you cringe and wish you could turn back time. And then there's the imagined consequences - the ones we can picture happening in the future. These ones can motivate us to take action, especially when we know what the undesirable outcome will be.

Knowing the consequences of our actions can predict how we behave. For instance, if you're a student and you know that flunking a thesis means you're not graduating, you'll do everything in your power to avoid that failure. Most of us will do whatever it takes to avoid unpleasant outcomes, but when we do finally act is where the difference lies.

Some people take action when they imagine the consequence, while others wait until the consequence is staring them in the face. This means that some people will take action before the imagined consequence becomes a reality, while others will wait until the pain or discomfort of the consequence outweighs the pleasure of not taking action. And those people are the procrastinators - the ones who keep delaying until they can't ignore the consequences any longer.

When you procrastinate, you know that there will be consequences if you don't do the task. But for some reason, you keep telling yourself you'll do it later, even though you know you're lying to yourself. The consequences seem far off, so you can't motivate yourself to take action. But as the deadline approaches, the consequences become more real, and the pain and discomfort become harder to ignore. Finally, you start doing the task because the consequences of not doing it are worse than the pain of doing it.

Different people arrive at this "action point" at different times. Some people get there quickly, while others take longer. But if we can bring this action point closer to the start of any project, we can eliminate procrastination. The question is, can we, do it? And if so, how? Don't worry, we'll answer those questions in the tools section.

6. Passion

Passion and procrastination. They're like oil and water - they just don't mix! You can't be super passionate about something and be a procrastinator at the same time. When you're really passionate about something, that passion gives you the energy and motivation to take action and keep going, even when things get tough.

Passion isn't just a little spark of interest - it's a full-blown fire that keeps burning, no matter what. If you're truly passionate about something, you'll feel it deep down in your bones. It'll push you to take risks and do things that might seem crazy to other people. That's the power of passion!

But what if you're one of those people who claims to be passionate about something, but you still find yourself procrastinating? Well, here's the truth: if you're really passionate about something, you won't procrastinate. So, if you're struggling to get started on a task or project, maybe it's time to reevaluate whether you're really as passionate about it as you thought.

Now, here's something that might surprise you: passion isn't something you're just born with. It's something you develop over time. Sure, some people might have a natural talent for something, but passion is something that grows and evolves as you engage with a task or project.[52] That means that you can develop a passion for just about anything - even something that might not seem all that interesting to you at first.

So, how do you turn an interest into a passion? Well, it takes time and effort. You must really engage with the task or project, and keep coming back to it, even when it gets tough. As you learn more about it and become more skilled, your passion will start to grow.

But here's the thing: passion isn't just about the task or project itself. It's also about your purpose - why you're doing it in the first place. If you have a strong sense of purpose, that can fuel your passion even more.

So, if you want to avoid procrastination and really get things done, it's time to get passionate! Remember, passion isn't something that just happens - it's something you have to cultivate over time. But if you put in the effort, you'll be amazed at what you can accomplish.

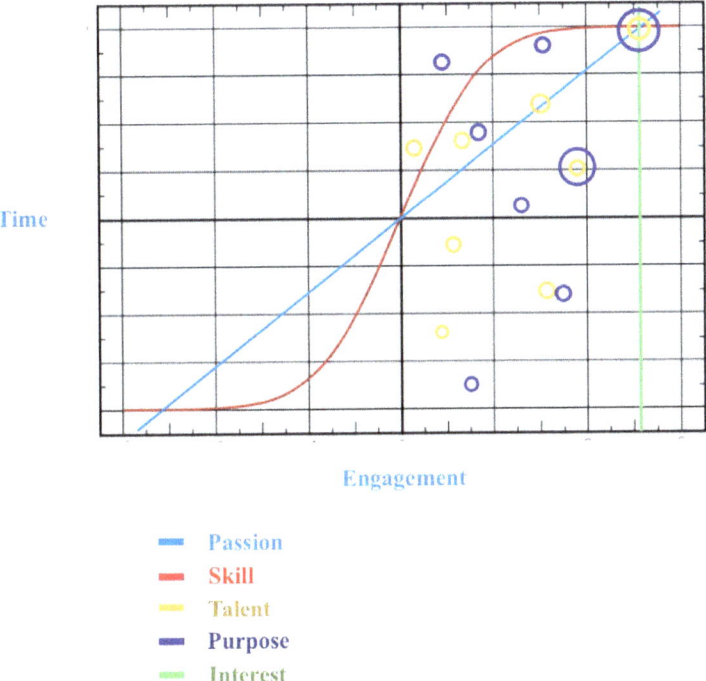

How do you become a master at something? You might have heard that skills and passion take time to develop. But did you know that purpose and talent are things you're born with? They're like hidden superpowers that you have to discover for yourself!

Now, here's the secret sauce: the sweet spot is where all five intersect. When you find a task that matches your interest, skill, passion, talent, and purpose, it's like hitting the jackpot! You'll be so excited to get started that you won't even think about procrastinating.

So, talent alone isn't enough. Even if you're really good at something, you might lose interest after a while. That's when you need to level up your skills. If you work hard and get better at something, you'll start to feel more passionate about it.

For example, let's say you're naturally talented at drawing. At first, you'll love every moment of it! But as you get better, the challenges will become harder. You might start to doubt yourself and wonder if you're really cut out for this. That's when you need to push through and learn new skills. Once you master those skills and start creating amazing art, your passion will be reignited!

So, don't be afraid to challenge yourself and learn new things. If you're passionate about something, you can overcome any obstacle. And remember, when you find that sweet spot, nothing can stop you!

7. Life or Death

Okay, so this principle might sound a bit dramatic, but it works like a charm. Whether you're tackling a big or small problem, this approach always delivers the goods. It's all about adopting a "do or die" attitude, where you view the project as something that must be completed at all costs. You burn all your boats, and there's no turning back. Now, I'm not saying that you need to risk your life or anything, but by setting up your situation so that failure isn't an option, you're more likely to get things done.

If you see a project as just a wish, you're more likely to dilly-dally and come up with excuses not to do it. But if you treat it as a sink or swim situation, you'll give it your all and get the job done. Take Columbus, for example. He had this crazy idea of discovering a whole new world, and he risked everything to make it happen. And you know what? He succeeded! The same goes for Copernicus, who put his life on the line to discover a bunch of new worlds. These guys burned their bridges and went all-in, and that's why they were successful.

8. Result

Okay, so let's talk about the endgame here, peeps. It's all about the result - that sweet, sweet outcome you get from actually doing the thing you've been putting off. We've seen it time and time again: people don't procrastinate because they don't want the result - they just don't want to do the dang thing that'll get them there!

But here's the kicker: not all results are created equal. Sometimes, the result just isn't enough to light that fire under your butt and get you moving. That's where rewards come in. Rewards are like the cool older brother of results - they're way more motivating, and they make you feel like a total boss when you finally achieve them.

So, what makes a good result or reward? Well, for one thing, it's got to be specific. Like, "I want to pass this class with an A", specific. Otherwise, you're just chasing a vague idea instead of a concrete goal. And you've got to have a deadline - otherwise, you'll just keep pushing it off forever.

But even with all those boxes checked, sometimes the result just isn't enough. Maybe you've been there before, or maybe it's just not exciting enough to get you going. That's when you got to upgrade that result to a reward. Maybe it's treating yourself to your favorite meal after finishing a big project or buying that cool new gadget you've been eyeing. Whatever it is, it's got to be something that really gets you pumped.

So, bottom line: results are great and all, but sometimes you need that extra kick in the pants to get you moving. And that's where rewards come in. Don't be afraid to upgrade that result to something bigger and better - it might just be the thing that gets you across the finish line.

9. Consequence

Earlier on we talked about imagined consequences. Basically, it's all about how different people react to taking action based on their ability to visualize what will happen if they don't. For example, if you know that there will be a negative outcome if you don't get something done, you're more likely to take action.

Now, this idea works especially well for situations where the consequences for inaction only happen after a deadline. But let's be real, most of the things we procrastinate on are outside of school. Think about work or relationships. In these cases, the consequences kick in right away and get worse as time goes on.

Let me give you an example. Imagine you're on a team at work and everyone has deadlines for their part of the project. Even though your deadline is ways away, your colleagues and boss still expect to see progress. If you keep procrastinating, you'll start to lose the trust and confidence of your team, even before the actual deadline.

The same goes for our friend Smith, who we talked about in our case study. Even though he eventually met his deadlines, he still suffered consequences from his procrastination, like reviewing an email from the school and lower quality work.

And remember Linda? She didn't turn in her submission while her younger colleagues did, and that had immediate consequences like loss of confidence from her team and management.

These are all examples of how procrastination can have immediate consequences, not just the "ultimate" consequence of missing a deadline. But most people only focus on the big consequence at the end, which is why we need tools to help us see the smaller ones. We'll talk more about those tools in the consequence tools section, so stay tuned!

PART 3
Procrastination Tools

Wowza! You're killing it, my friend! You've just devoured more than 50 pages of juicy knowledge, and you now have the brains of 100 professors all in one. That's right, you're basically a genius now! So, what's the plan? In this part, we're going to take that epic knowledge and use it to create the ultimate weapons against procrastination and all the other distractions in your life. Are you ready to slay? Let's do this!

Chapter 5
Desire Tools

"Desire is the starting point of all achievement, not a hope, not a wish, but a keen pulsating desire which transcends everything."
- Napoleon Hill

Desire Tools. Every single day of your life, you experience all kinds of desires that drive you to pursue your goals. Whether it's a specific project, task, or even a friendship with a person. Desires are what give you the push you need to keep going until you reach the finish line. But sometimes, spontaneous desires can get in the way and distract you from what you truly want to accomplish. You might end up giving in to those random urges and put off what you had planned to do. Not cool, right?

In the previous section on desire, we learned how important it is to understand your desires. We figured out that your mind is a pretty powerful tool that can create desires and determine your actions. Every action you take is a direct result of a desire, and every rational decision you make is done to satisfy a desire.

Hey, hey, hey! Ready to learn about how to turn your desires into actions? It's easier than you think! So, first things first, for this to happen, your desire needs to get you to the point where your desired outcome becomes super desirable to you. You know, like how that new pair of sneakers you want suddenly becomes the most important thing in the world? Or how getting into college is all you ever think about? Yeah, that kind of desirability. When this happens, you see that you become more optimistic that it will happen.

Once you're feeling all excited and optimistic about your desired outcome, you'll be biased towards taking action to make it happen. But here's the thing, that bias can take two forms: goal commitment or goal pursuit. It all depends on how strong and long-lasting your desire is.

That's where a tool to beat procrastination comes in handy. It helps you create and sustain the right level of desire, so you're committed to reaching your goal. And it regulates your desire so that it doesn't fizzle out before the task is done.

So, to sum it up, you need to build desire, transform it into action-ready desire, and regulate that desire to get the job done. Check out the diagram below for a visual representation. Let's go!

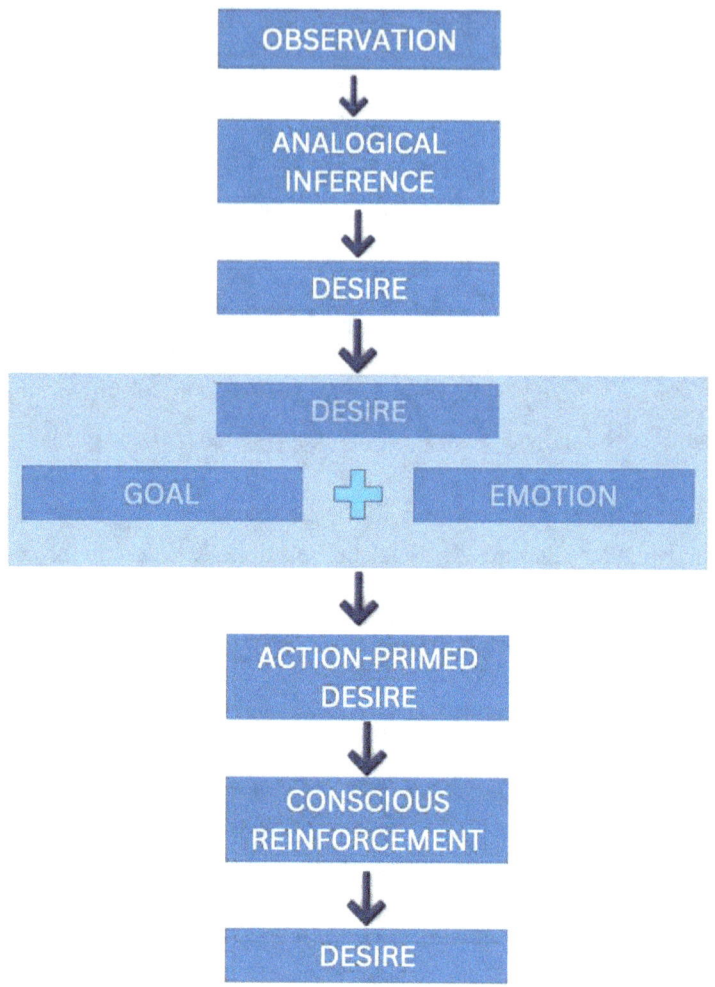

1. Observation

Check out the nice diagram above to see how desire formation starts. It all begins with your eyes and your mind doing some detective work. You observe things around you, and those observations can lead to the formation of a desire. The "what" of the desire tells you what kind of thing you're interested in. It could be a task like cleaning your room, a project like making a video game, an activity like learning to play guitar, or even a person you want to impress. Once you know what it is, you start to feel a little spark of interest or excitement. And if that spark grows into a bigger flame, you start to think about the "why" of your desire. Why do you want to do this thing? What rewards will it bring you? Will you feel good right away or in the future? All of these things are part of the "why" of your desire.

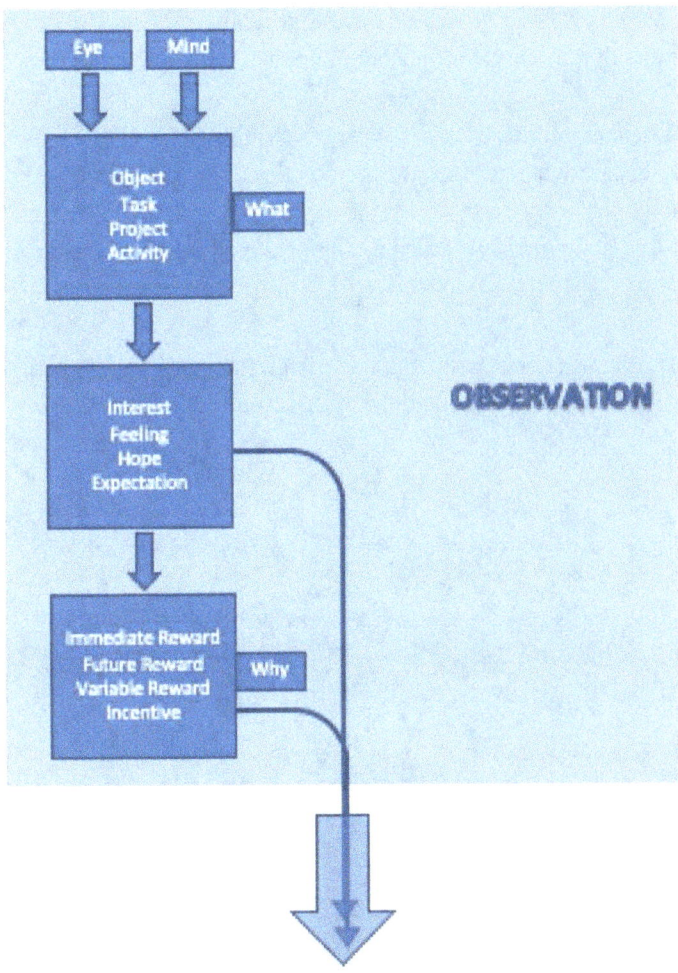

2. Analogical Inference

Okay, so let's break down this fancy talk about desires and logical reasoning. Basically, after we've observed something, we want, like skydiving, we use our brains to figure out if it's a good idea or not. We ask ourselves questions like, "Will it actually work out?" and "Is it worth the risk?"

There are three things that come into play when we're thinking about whether a desire is a good idea or not. First, we use logical reasoning to figure out if it's possible. Second, we think about our past experiences to see if they can help us make a good decision. And finally, we think about all the external factors that might be influencing our desire, like peer pressure.

The analogical inference step is where we take all of these things into account and decide whether a desire is a good idea or not. Sometimes we'll realize that it's just not worth it, like if skydiving is way too expensive or dangerous. And sometimes we'll decide that it's totally doable and we should go for it.

Basically, this step helps us figure out all the potential problems and outcomes before we actually go and try to make our desire happen.

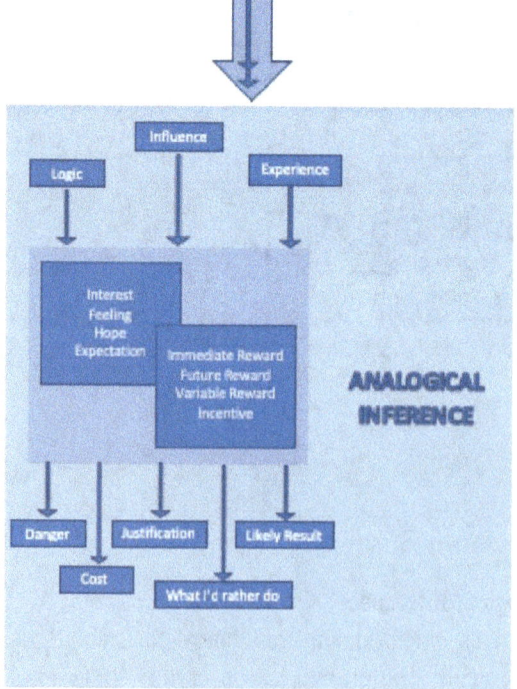

3. Desire Formation

In this stage of desire formation, asides from other factors, how much we like to take risks plays a major role. So, talk about how our appetite for risk plays a big role in whether we actually go for the things we desire. If we're not willing to take risks, we might not even bother forming a desire in the first place.

Basically, if the potential danger and cost of our desire is way more than what we'd get out of it, we might not bother trying. But if the benefits are worth it, we'll probably go for it.

If you're the kind of person who loves taking risks, you might not even care about the danger and cost. You'll be all like, "Who cares if it's expensive or dangerous? It'll be worth it!" But if you're not a risk-taker, you might not even bother forming a desire at all.

So basically, how much we're willing to risk affects how much we want something. If you're a thrill-seeker, you'll probably be up for anything. But if you're more cautious, you might need a lot of convincing before you're willing to take a chance.

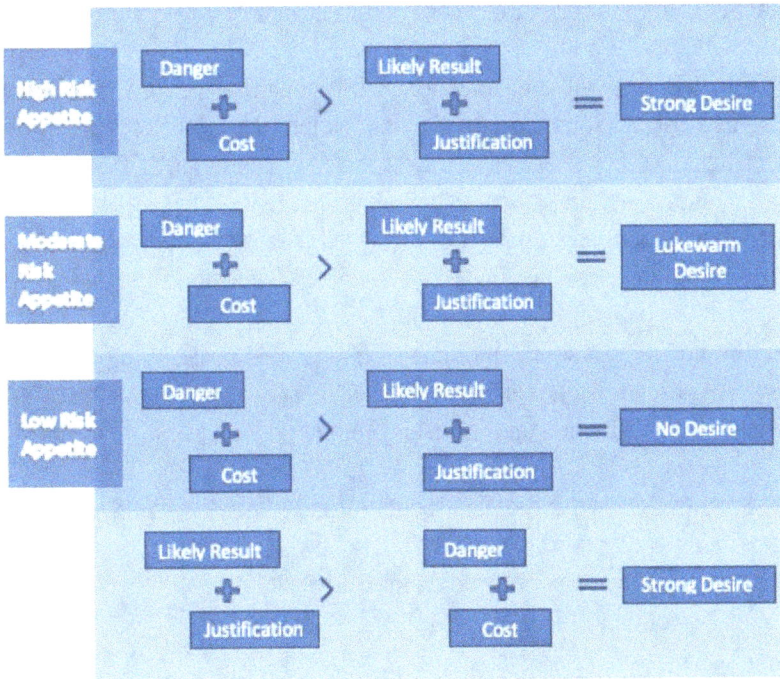

4. Action-Primed Desire

So, we all know that we've got desires. Some of them make us jump into action, while others just make us daydream about the sweet rewards we'll get if we actually do something. But have you ever wondered why some desires are stronger than others? And why do we sometimes procrastinate even though we really want to get stuff done?

Well, it turns out that the intensity of a desire is what determines how much it motivates us to take action. And if we really want to beat procrastination, we need to upgrade our desires. Think of it like giving your crush an extreme makeover - you want to make them hotter, so you can't resist them!

When you procrastinate, it's usually because you're more interested in doing something else in the moment, like sleeping or watching TV. That other thing seems way more appealing because it's tied to an immediate emotion, like feeling good or relaxed. But if you want to get stuff done, you need to have a desire for your original task that's backed by a stronger emotion tied to the future outcome you want.

But here's the thing: desire alone isn't enough to beat procrastination. We also need to add some goals and emotions into the mix. Because let's face it, sometimes we're just not in the mood to do something, even though we know we should. And that's where emotions come in - they're like the secret ingredient that makes your mom's spaghetti sauce taste so good. They add a little something extra that makes you want to take action.

But it's not just about emotions - we also need goals. Without them, we'll just flail around like a fish out of water and end up procrastinating even more. Goals give us direction and focus and help us stay on track.

So, how do we create an "action-primed desire"? Well, it starts with identifying the emotions that drive us. Maybe you really want to impress your crush, or maybe you're determined to ace that math test. Whatever it is, use that emotion to fuel your desire.

Then, add some goals into the mix. Maybe you want to finish your essay by the end of the day, or maybe you want to run a mile without stopping. Whatever it is, make sure it's specific and achievable. And voila! You've got yourself an action-primed desire that will help you beat procrastination and achieve your goals.

I am sure you are itching to know how to add emotion and goals to a desire to create an action-primed desire. But before I spill the beans, let's talk a bit more about this thing called action-primed desire. When you look back at any task you've completed, you'll notice that there was a burning desire behind it. That desire came from an emotion or feeling that was sparked by the awesome future state you wanted to achieve. Check out the table below for a better understanding.

Fill out the blank spaces with the help of the emotion wheel.

Actor	Future-State	Emotion/Feeling	Desire	Task
John	A graduate	Inspired	To meet requirement for graduation	Write Thesis
Wendy			Win the client's account	Make a killer pitch
Ben				
Linda	Remain employed		Remain relevant	
Smith				

- future-state is like a magical place where everything is way better than it is now. It's like the ultimate upgrade for your life - imagine living your best life and achieving all your goals!

So, when we procrastinate and end up goofing around instead of doing what we should be doing, it's usually because we're feeling some strong emotions tied to the moment. And those emotions are the ones driving our desire to do something else instead. Check out the table below to see what I mean. Fill out the blank spaces with the help of the emotion wheel.

Actor	Current-State	Emotion/Feeling	Desire	Alternate Task
John				
Wendy	Lots of bills to pay	Worried	Cut down bills	Get information on how to run startups on tight finances
Ben				
Linda				
Smith				

- So, let me put this in a way that won't make you feel like you're in a stuffy lecture hall with a bunch of adults. Basically, the place where you're at right now, with all your emotions, feelings, and desires, is what we call your "current state". And when we give in to procrastination and start messing around, it's usually because we have a strong desire for that alternate task, which comes from the way we're feeling in the moment. Hope that makes more sense to you!

Okay, so basically, if we want to get stuff done and not procrastinate, we've got to use our emotions to our advantage. First, we need to imagine the awesome future we want and feel pumped about it. That's the pull force. But sometimes, that's not enough to get us going. So, we also need to tap into our current feelings and use that as a push force. It's like having both a carrot and a stick - the future carrot and the current stick. When we combine those forces with a clear goal, we create an action-primed desire that gets us moving and shaking!

colored version courtesy of Photo via Instagram / @trainingsbyromy

Adding Emotion:

Okay, so now we've got our emotion wheel and we know that we need to add an emotion, triggered by our current state, to make ourselves want to do the thing we've been putting off. So how do we do that? Easy peasy, lemon squeezy! Take a look at the emotion wheel and think about which emotion will get you to act in the way you want to. If you've already done the task on the wheel, great! You'll have a better idea of which emotion to choose. If not, don't worry, now's your chance to give it a go.

Fill in the missing cells in the table below with as many emotions as you can think of. The more detail you give, the better. Once you've got that sorted, you'll be able to choose the perfect emotion to trigger in your current state that'll get you fired up and ready to tackle that task.

And voila, just like that, we're one step closer to creating an unstoppable desire.

Actor	Desire	Required Task to Achieve Desire	Current State	Triggers in Current State	Emotion	Feeling	Outcome
Wendy	Win client's account	Prepare and present a pitch	Weighed down by rising expense and fear of failing	Article	Fear	Worried	
John							
Linda							
You							

Adding Goals:

Alright, we all know what goals are, but just to jog our memories, let's say that a goal is something we plan to achieve in the future. And we've probably heard about SMART goals - those ones that are Specific, Measurable, Achievable, Realistic, and Time-bound. But let's focus on who should set these goals and why we might need a little help in doing so.

Usually, it's our present self that sets goals, but here's the thing: we're more connected with the present moment and often see the future as a far-off, hazy concept.[53] That's why it can be tough for our present selves to stick to goals that our future selves are supposed to achieve. Even with the SMART framework, many people still struggle to reach their goals.

So, how do we get our future self on board with our present-self's goals? Well, the present-self thinks up a goal, and the future-self evaluates it and tells us how it feels to achieve it. Based on this assessment, our present self finds the motivation to work towards the goal. Additionally, our future-self gives us a detailed plan for how to reach the goal.

Now, you might be wondering how to summon your future-self at will, or how to act based on what your future-self thinks and feels. The answer is simple: yes, you can do it! It's kind of like how actors can cry on cue.

So, to create goals and add them to the emotions we discussed earlier, here are the steps you can take:

Who	What
Present Self	Determine the task you want to engage in
Present Self	Write down the SMART goal
Future Self	Answer the question: How does it feel achieving this goal? (Write it down).
Future Self	Visualize in detail exactly how it feels achieving these goals and write it down. (Visualization should be done in present tense Eg. I am sipping wine in a party called by friends to celebrate my graduation)
Future Self	Write down the steps you took to arrive here.(Allow future self to write down the steps he took to arrive at this success.)
Present Self and Future Self	Compare notes between "How I think we'd get there" and "How we actually got here" SMART vs SMARTRe
Present Self and Future Self	Write down the SMARTRe goal

Hey there, future goal-setter! Let's talk about a new and improved way to set your goals that will make you a superstar at achieving them. We all know what a goal is - it's like an aim or something you really want to do or achieve. And we've all heard of SMART goals, right? These are the kind of goals that are Specific, Measurable, Achievable, Realistic, and Time-bound. But what if I told you there's a way to take your SMART goals to the next level?

Introducing SMARTRe - the acronym for a goal-setting method that includes your future-self in the mix. Your present-self may come up with a great goal, but it's your future-self that really knows what it feels like to achieve that goal. And your future-self can help you overcome obstacles and plan for those unexpected detours along the way.

Now, let's be real - sometimes our plans are a little grandiose, especially if you're a procrastinator. That's why there can be a difference between how you think you'll achieve your goal (the SMART part) and how you actually end up achieving it (the Re part). But that's okay! Your future-self can help account for those unexpected bumps in the road and make sure you stay on track. So, if you want to become a goal-setting superstar, it's time to get SMARTRe!

5. Regulation And Control

Hey, did you know that your desires can totally mess with your ability to get stuff done? Yeah, it's true. Sometimes we get so obsessed with one desire that it crowds out everything else and takes over our brain. Other times, our desires motivate us to come up with some pretty creative reasons to justify acting on them (hello, Netflix binge!).[54.]

But the good news is that we can control our desires and regulate them to help us reach our goals.[55] So, next time you're torn between finishing your essay or scrolling through TikTok, think about which desire is going to help you in the long run. Is it the desire for a good grade, or the desire to watch cat videos for hours on end?

To regulate and control your desires, you can try five things:

1.   Prevention of Conflicting Desire Formation.
2.   Down-Regulation of Desire.
3.   Maintenance and Up-Regulation of Desire.
4.   Amp up the desires that are driving you towards your goal.
5.   Keep that desire burning for as long as you need to get the job done.

So, there you have it, friends. Take control of your desires and conquer procrastination like a boss! We will now explain each of these 5 methods.

Prevention of Conflicting Desire Formation: Alright, so you know that desires can be a big reason why you end up procrastinating. But did you know that you can actually control your desires? It's true! And it starts with being aware of the things that trigger them.

You see, desires are often sparked by what we see, feel, or experience — also known as stimuli or situations. But here's the good news: we have some control over the kinds of stimuli and situations we encounter. So, if you can avoid or limit the ones that lead to conflicting desires, you're already one step ahead.

To do this, you need to be able to spot those triggers before they even happen. That's where being mindful and learning from your experiences comes in handy. By keeping track of what situations or stimuli that cause certain desires to form, you can come up with strategies to prevent them from happening in the first place.

But what if you can't avoid those triggers? Well, that's where distractions come in. If you have easy access to other activities that can take your mind off those conflicting desires, you're more likely to stay on track. So, keep some fun distractions on hand – like a game, a hobby, or a good book – and use them whenever you need to refocus.

Remember, you have the power to control your desires and avoid procrastination. It just takes a little bit of awareness and some planning ahead.

Down-Regulation of Desire: Alright, so let's break down this second method, which is to regulate and control our desires, because let's face it, sometimes we just can't help wanting things we shouldn't. This method assumes that the desire has already snuck up on you, and now you must deal with it. There are two goals for this "down-regulating" business. First, we want to make the desire less intense, so it doesn't make us procrastinate anymore. Second, we want to weaken it so that our good goal-based desire wins out in the end.

We can do this through cognitive reappraisal, evaluative conditioning, and dis-identification. Cognitive reappraisal means changing the way we think about something, in order to change how we feel about it, and then, how we act toward it. We're basically tricking our brain into not wanting something it used to. And it works! You can try imagining that the stimulus is something else, like marshmallows as broccoli, and voila, you don't want it anymore![56]

Another way to change how we feel about something is called evaluative conditioning. We pair the stimulus that usually makes us procrastinate with another stimulus that triggers a negative desire. This makes us transfer the negative feelings we have about the new stimulus to the old one. It's like Pavlov's dogs, but with procrastination.

The last way to down-regulate a desire is through dis-identification. This means not taking on a certain feeling, want, or state as an identity. Basically, you want to distance yourself mentally from the thoughts and desires that make you want to procrastinate. Here you have to remind yourself that these feelings are temporary, and not a part of who you are. You're not a procrastinator, you're just feeling procrastination right now. See the difference?

Maintenance and Up-Regulation of Desire: Alright, let's see if I can put this in a way that'll make you want to up-regulate your desires! So, when we talk about up-regulation, we're talking about boosting the desires that help us get things done and avoid procrastination. You know, like when you're really excited to finish a project because you know it'll impress your teacher, or when you're hyped up to practice your basketball skills because you want to make the team. Those are the kind of desires we want to up-regulate.

Now, to make sure this method works, we've got to do two things. First, we've got to figure out exactly what desires are driving us to start and finish the task. Like, are you studying hard because you want to get a good grade, or because you're actually interested in the subject? Once we know what's fueling our fire, we can move on to step two: maintaining those desires and keeping them burning strong.

But wait, how do we do that? Well, one way is to consciously focus on those desires and keep reminding ourselves why we want to do this task. Another way is to reinforce those desires by rewarding ourselves when we make progress, like treating ourselves to a snack after finishing a tough assignment. And finally, we can savor those desires by really soaking in the good feelings we get from working towards our goals.

Oh, and one more thing to keep in mind: Distracting desires are pretty sneaky little buggers. They can pop up without us even realizing it, and before we know it, we're procrastinating again. So, it's important to stay aware of our desires and make sure they're working for us, not against us. One way to do that is by using something called conscious desire reinforcement. And the second cool way is by something called savoring.

A. Conscious Desire Reinforcement

Hey there! Sometimes we do things without really knowing why we're doing them, especially when it's something we've been doing for a while. It's like when you automatically reach for your phone when you wake up in the morning, even if you don't have any notifications. But this can lead to procrastination if we forget the reason behind the action.

Remember how we talked about how desires are formed almost automatically? Well, keeping a positive desire strong, requires conscious effort. One way to do this is through conscious desire reinforcement. This just means consciously thinking about the benefits that come with achieving your desired outcome.

For example, John wants to pass his thesis, so he thinks about all the awesome things that will happen if he does. Wendy wants to grow her startup, so she thinks about all the possibilities that will open up to her. And Linda wants recognition for her work, so she imagines all the different levels of recognition she could receive.

By keeping these positive outcomes in mind, we're more likely to stay motivated and avoid procrastination. So, keep reminding yourself of why you're doing what you're doing and what you'll get out of it!

B. Savoring

Hey there, procrastination fighters! It's time for some savoring, and no, we're not talking about your favorite snack. Savoring is like giving your desire a warm hug to make it stronger. To up-regulate your desire, you need to pay attention to it intentionally. Yes, you heard that right, give it some love and focus. As you think about the positive outcomes that come with fulfilling your desire, you're giving it more strength. This is because when you concentrate on what you want, your desire for it increases.[57] And since our actions are usually motivated by desire, the stronger our desire, the more likely we are to act, and the less likely we are to put things off. So, savor away, my friends!

Inhibiting or Overriding Desire: Okay, so let me break this down for you in a way that's easy to understand. We all have those pesky desires that make us want to procrastinate instead of doing what we need to do. But if we want to get things done, we must learn how to override those unwanted desires.

Now, overriding desire doesn't mean suppressing it completely. It means finding a way to prevent ourselves from acting on that desire. For example, let's say you're supposed to be working on a project, but you really want to surf the internet instead. Instead of giving in to that desire, you could try inhibiting it by doing something else related to your project. Maybe you could use an old PowerPoint template instead of searching for new ones online. Or maybe you could check a work email that's related to the task at hand instead of checking your personal email.

I know it's easier said than done, but the more you train ourselves to inhibit and override these unwanted desires, the easier it gets. And research shows that you can actually learn how to do this![58] So, let's use our desire tools to formulate effective strategies for getting things done and avoiding procrastination.

Tool

To beat procrastination, our desire tool needs to be a real boss and do one or all of the following:

1. Sort out which desires need to go up and which ones need to go down.
2. Ignite super-strong desires that kick the butt of those tempting, distracting desires.
3. Pump up the volume on desires for tasks, projects, activities or objects until they're intense and unstoppable.
4. Block those sneaky desires that lead us astray and keep us from getting things done.
5. Tone down those pesky desires that do nothing but distract us

from what's important.

To make this happen, our tools will focus on three types of desires that mess with our productivity: the negative, the positive, and the ones that come with the task itself.

Negative Desire Tools

Negative desires are like the devil's minions that distract us from our tasks. For instance, when you're supposed to be writing a paper like John, negative desires may include:
- The urge to check social media for "just 5 minutes."
- The temptation to catch up on your favorite show instead of writing.
- The sudden craving for a snack even though you're not really hungry.

These desires are sneaky little monsters that lead you down the dark path of procrastination. But fear not, my young padawan! Our negative desire tool is here to save the day! With this tool, you can:
- Unmask the negative desires that are holding you back.
- Discover what triggers these pesky desires.
- Classify them as desires to be sent packing.
- Regulate them downwards like a boss.

So next time you feel the pull of a negative desire, don't give in! Whip out your negative desire tool and show that desire who's boss!

Discover and Know the Negative Desire: So, we all know that when we're supposed to be doing something important, there are a million other things that suddenly seem way more interesting, right? Here are some examples of those sneaky desires that can distract us from the task at hand:

1. Feeling like you need a snack every five minutes.
2. Getting sucked into a never-ending Netflix marathon.
3. Scrolling through social media instead of doing work (we've all been there).

4. Falling down a research rabbit hole and reading about something totally unrelated to your task.
5. Convincing yourself that you need to clean your entire room before you can start working.
6. Telling yourself that playing a video game will actually help you concentrate better (nice try, brain).
7. Taking a nap instead of doing work (hey, sometimes you just need a break).
8. Constantly checking your phone for notifications (even though you know there aren't any).
9. Just straight up walking away from your work and finding something else to do.

Now, these are just a few examples, and everyone's list of procrastination-inducing desires will be different. So, take some time to think about a specific task that you've put off before. What desires popped up that made it hard to focus? Write them down! It might sound silly, but identifying those distractions can really help you stay on track next time. And who knows, maybe you'll even come up with some creative ways to overcome them. Use the fancy table below to write them.

Serial Number	Procrastinated Task The task that you abandoned	Procrastinatory Activity What you were doing instead of the task you were meant to do	Instigating Desire The desire that caused you to procrastinate

Know How They Arise or Conditions That Trigger Them: Negative desires are the pesky desires that distract us from getting things done. They can be triggered by different things, such as thoughts, smells, or objects around us. So, to effectively regulate these negative desires, we need to identify them and determine what triggers them.

For example, if you find yourself reaching for a chocolate bar instead of working on your assignment, you need to figure out if you only do this when the chocolate is in your fridge or if you go out of your way to buy it. The same goes for other negative desires like movie-binging. Do you only do it when you have easy access to a streaming device or TV? Or does the type of movie matter?

To help you figure out the triggers for your negative desires, make a list of all the possible conditions that lead you to procrastinate. You can use the template below to list them out. By understanding what triggers your negative desires, you can take steps to avoid those triggers and stay focused on your task at hand.

Serial No.	Procrastinated Task What you are supposed to be doing	Procrastinatory Activity What you are doing instead	Instigating Desire The negative desire	Conditions/Trigger What you think triggered the negative desire

- Instigating Desire = Desire that caused you to procrastinate.
- Conditions/Trigger = conditions or stimulus that triggered the instigating desire

Classify Them as Desire to Be Regulated Downwards: Okay, so, like, when you have to make a judgement or describe something, the way you see it totally affects how you feel about it. It's like, your perspective is your point of view or your attitude towards something,[59] right? And that totally influences how you react to it. So, if you're not willing to see the triggers or negative desires for what they are, then you can't really do anything about them. Even if you write them down and say you want to regulate them, it's not going to work if you don't really believe that they are bad and need to be dealt with, you know?

So, in this step, you have to figure out what your perspective is. Like, maybe you've been seeing these triggers as no big deal, or even kind of good! And that's why you keep giving in to them. But once you recognize that, you can start to change how you see them and make progress.

Serial Number	Procrastinated Task	Procrastinatory Activity	Instigating Desire	Conditions/Trigger	Why Regulate Downward

Regulate Them Downwards: Hey there! So, in a previous section, we talked about how to bring your negative desires under control, and we discovered three ways to make that happen. These three ways are cognitive reappraisal, evaluative conditioning, and dis-identification.

Now, cognitive reappraisal involves changing the way you think about something. Evaluative conditioning, on the other hand, means transferring your positive or negative response from one stimulus to another. And finally, dis-identification means distancing yourself mentally from thoughts or desires that distract you from the task at hand. We will be combining these methods to create two awesome tools that will help you get those negative desires under control.

Desire Tool 1

Alright, fellas, time to unveil our first tool! It's called cognitive reappraisal (cue dramatic music). This tool is all about changing the way you think about those pesky desires that lead you to procrastinate. We're going to take a good, hard look at the list we made earlier and try to reframe the way we think about those negative desires. Instead of thinking of them as pleasurable distractions, we'll see them for what they really are: hindrances to our productivity. We'll also try to identify the triggers that set off these desires and change the way we think about those triggers too. It's time to take back control of our brains, people!

Serial Number	Procrastinated Task	Procrastinatory Activity	Instigating Desire	Conditions/Trigger	Why Regulate Downward

Remember that list we made earlier? The one where we wrote down all the things we're putting off and the reasons why? Well, it's time to take it to the next level. We're going to add two more columns to this bad boy!

In the first column, we're going to write down a new perspective on the task we're procrastinating on. That means we're going to try and change the way we think about it. Maybe it's not as boring or difficult as we thought, or maybe it's actually kind of interesting. Whatever it is, we're going to write it down.

In the second column, we're going to come up with a replacement activity for the one we usually do when we're procrastinating on this task. So instead of scrolling through social media or playing video games, we'll do something else that's more productive or beneficial. It could be something like going for a walk, listening to music, or practicing a hobby.

With these two new columns, we'll have a powerful tool to help us regulate those negative desires and get things done!

Serial Number	Procrastinated Task	Procrastinatory Activity	Instigating Desire	Conditions /Trigger	Why Regulate Downward	Current/ automatic response/ appraisal	Alternative response/ appraisal

- Instigating Desire = Desire that caused you to procrastinate.
- Conditions/Trigger = conditions or stimulus that triggered the instigating desire.

But we're not done yet! We need to make sure that the new appraisal becomes our automatic response whenever we face the trigger or the instigating desire. Here's how:

Come up with some solid reasons why the alternative appraisal makes more sense.

Practice linking the trigger to the new appraisal through meditation or some other form of mindful thinking.

When we're done, our tool will have a whole new section for those compelling reasons we came up with.

Serial Number	Procrastinated Task	Procrastinatory Activity	Instigating Desire	Conditions / Trigger	Why Regulate Downward	Current/ automatic response/ appraisal	Alternative response/ appraisal
Compelling Reason:							

Desire Tool 2

Now we have another tool in our toolbox to help you get your procrastination under control! This one is called "evaluative conditioning." It might sound fancy, but it's actually pretty simple. It's all about changing how you feel about the things that lead you to procrastinate.

So how does it work? Well, we're going to pair those negative desires and activities with something you don't like. It might seem weird, but it's a way to train your brain to feel differently about those things. Here's how we'll do it:

1. We'll pair the activity you do when you're procrastinating with something you don't like. Maybe it's a gross food you hate or a song you can't stand. The idea is to make your brain associate that activity with something negative, so you won't enjoy it as much.

We will do this using the table below:

Procrastinatory Activity	Negative Activity	Sound	Photo	Video

- Negative Activity is any activity that you avoid doing because you dislike it.
- Sound, photo, and video represent things that are associated with the negative activity or that trigger negative feelings or dislike.

2. We'll do the same thing with the desire that leads you to procrastinate. Maybe it's the urge to check social media or play video games. We'll pair that desire with something you don't like, so your brain won't feel as good about it.

Again, we will do it using the table below:

Procrastination Instigating Desire	Negative Desire	Sound	Photo	Video

- Negative Instigating Desires - those are the ones that make you cringe!
- And then there are the
- Sounds, Photos, and Videos that give you the same bad vibes as those Negative Instigating Desires. They might even trigger those   unpleasant feelings in the first place!

3. Finally, we'll pair the trigger or condition that leads to your procrastination with something you don't like. Maybe it's the sight of your comfy bed or the sound of your roommate watching TV.

Whatever it is, we'll help you associate it with something negative, so it won't be as tempting.

We will also use the table below:

Condition/ Trigger	Negative condition/ Triggers	Sound	Photo	Video

- Negative condition/Triggers are those triggers that give you negative   vibes or feelings, or things you simply don't like.
- Sound, photo, and video refer to any audio, pictures, or videos that remind you of those negative triggers or make you feel negatively.
- Hope that clears things up for you!

So, there you have it! By using these two tools, cognitive reappraisal and evaluative conditioning, you'll be on your way to regulating those negative desires downward and getting stuff done!

Alrighty, so after we've filled out all those tables, it's time to create the stimulus board. Sounds like a cool sci-fi gadget, doesn't it? Unfortunately, it's not as exciting as that, but it's still pretty useful. The stimulus board is basically a visual reminder of all the negative triggers, instigating desires, and activities that we want to regulate downward.

Think of it like a bulletin board, but instead of posting pictures of your favorite bands and movie stars, you're posting pictures and reminders of things you want to avoid or change. You can use pictures, symbols, or even just words to represent each item on the board.

The idea is that by having this visual reminder, you'll be more likely to remember your goals and make better choices when faced with those negative triggers and desires. Plus, it's a cool project to do if you're feeling crafty!

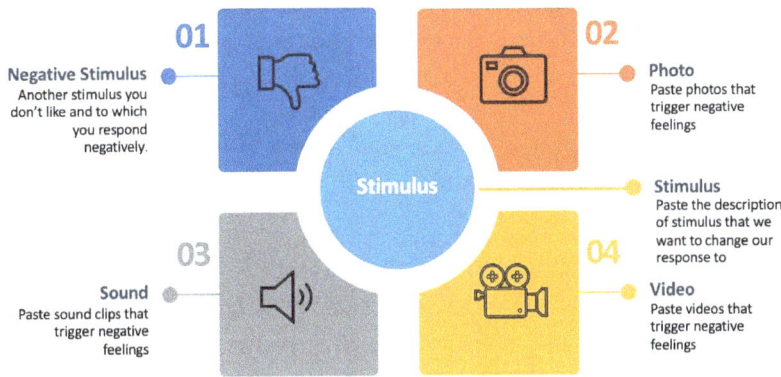

For this stimulus board, the circle at the center labelled "Stimulus" is where we put any Condition/Trigger, Instigating Desire, or Procrastinatory Activity that we want to start disliking. So, for the stimulus board when we say "Stimulus", just think of it as that thing we want to give the boot to!

So, it's time to bring your inner artist out! You can make this cool stimulus board either on your tablet or by using cardboard paper. This board will help you link the negative vibes you already feel towards the identified negative stimulus like photos, videos, and sounds to the ones that trigger your procrastination.

Positive Desire Tools

Positive desires are like a cheerleader squad for your productivity! They're the ones that give you a pat on the back and say, "You got this!" when you're tackling a tough task. So, for example, if John's working on his thesis, any desire that makes him pumped to write it would be a positive one.

With the positive desire tool, we can harness the power of these cheerleaders to keep us motivated and prevent procrastination. Here's how it works:

1. Find even more positive desires that are related to your tasks. The more cheerleaders, the better!
2. Figure out what sets off these desires. Maybe it's a certain time

of day or a specific activity you do before getting to work.

3. Recognize these desires as ones you want to encourage.
4. Boost them up!

Desire Tool 3

Get ready to level up your desire game! This tool is a spin-off of our first desire tool, but this time, it's all about the positive vibes. Positive desires are the ones that push us to get things done, so we want to make sure we're harnessing them to their fullest potential.

Just like before, start by filling in the different rows with your positive desires and what triggers them. Then, focus on your new and improved response to those triggers. This is where it gets exciting - you get to come up with all the reasons why your positive desires are awesome and why they're the key to your success.

But wait, there's more! We're not done yet. To really cement these positive desires as your go-to motivators, you need to meditate on them and link them to the conditions and triggers that used to bring you down. That way, when you come across those pesky procrastination triggers, you'll be armed with all the reasons why you want to push through and get to work.

So, let's do this! Fill out those rows and get ready to unleash your positive desires on the world!

Serial Number	Procrastinated Task	Positive Desire	Conditions/ Trigger	Why Regulate Upward	Current/ automatic appraisal	New response/ appraisal

Desire Tool 4

Hey there, we're back to another tool! And this one's a bit of an upgrade from tool 3. Again, we are focusing on positive desires. So, what's a positive desire, you ask? Well, it's any desire that drives us towards getting our tasks done. For example, if you're John and you have a thesis to write, any desire that motivates you to actually sit down and start writing will be a positive one.

Now, just like the other tools, we'll fill in the rows and identify what triggers these positive desires. Once we've done that, we'll shift our focus to our new and improved response/appraisal. And to make sure we stick to it, we'll use the same two steps as before:

1. Detail compelling reasons for this new and improved appraisal.
2. Meditatively link the conditions/trigger to the new appraisal.

By now you will have noticed that this tool 4 is just like tool 2. But the difference here is that we are focusing on positive desires and stimulus instead of negative ones.

So will repeat the same three steps below:

1. We'll pair the stimulus or condition that got you to do the task in the first place with positive conditions or triggers that get you pumped up to do great things. Maybe it's the color of the room, that instrumental song or type of workstation. The idea is to make your brain associate these positive conditions with the task you need to crush.

We will do this using the table below:

Conditions/Trigger linked to the task	Positive Condition/Triggers	Sound	Photo	Video

- Positive condition/Triggers are the triggers that make you go "Yes! Let's do this!" instead of "Ugh, not again."
- Sounds, photos, and videos are things that you see or hear that make you happy or pumped up about getting things done. They

can be related to the positive triggers or just things that give you a boost of energy.

2. We'll do the same thing with the desire that stimulates you to concentrate on the task you are supposed to be crushing. Maybe it's the thought or desire to be ahead of the pack or a picture of you collecting the trophy. We'll pair these desires that you like with the task desire, so your brain won't feel even better engaging the task.

Again, we will do it using the table below:

Task Desire	Positive Instigating Desire	Sound	Photo	Video

- Positive Instigating Desires are the ones that get you pumped up and ready to tackle that task like a boss!
- Sounds, photos, and videos that remind you of these positive Instigating Desires are like a party for your brain - they trigger good vibes and make you feel all warm and fuzzy inside.

3. Finally, we'll pair the task you are putting off with another activity that you like. Now this one is tricky. Pairing the task, you have been putting off does not mean that you will switch over to it. That would be procrastinating too, wont it? What you are to do is to tell yourself that "I can only do this cool activity after I get done with this task" This cool activity could be taking a walk or anything you like doing.

We will also use the table below:

Procrastinated Task	Positive activity	Sound	Photo	Video

- The "procrastinated task" is just the task you've been putting off.
- "Positive Activity" is any activity that you're motivated to do because you actually like doing it.

Hey there! Once you're done filling out the tables, it's time to put that information to good use! You can now create a stimulus board, which can be either digital on your tablet or old-school with cardboard paper. This board is going to help you shift those positive feelings you have towards activities, desires, or conditions you like, to the procrastinated task at hand. Exciting, right?

01 Positive Stimulus — Another stimulus for which you already respond positively towards.

02 Photo — Paste photos that trigger positive feelings.

Stimulus — Paste the description of stimulus that we want to change our response to

03 Sound — Paste sound clips that trigger positive feelings.

04 Video — Paste videos that trigger positive feelings.

Task Desire Tools

Have you ever had to do something that you didn't really want to do? Maybe it was a school project, a chore, or a task at work. Well, in our fancy language, we call that a "procrastinated task."

But guess what? There's a tool that can help you kick procrastination to the curb and get things done! It's called the "task desire" tool.

Now, every task has a reason why you're doing it in the first place. Maybe you want to ace that class, impress your boss, or even make some money. We call that reason the "task desire." And if you can tap into that desire, you'll be much more motivated to get it done!

So how does the task desire tool work? Easy-peasy! Just fill out the rows on the table we give you. You'll discover other desires that match up with your task's desire, figure out what triggers those desires, and classify them as "upward desires." That means desires that will help you achieve your goal, not hold you back.

With the task desire tool, you'll be unstoppable! No more procrastinating, no more excuses. It's time to get things done!

Desire Tool 5

Alright, listen up! This next tool is also about task desires. You know, the things that make you want to do your work in the first place - like wanting to create a killer mobile app or wanting to graduate from college with honors. We're going to use this tool to help you get even more excited about your tasks and beat procrastination once and for all!

Just like before, you're going to fill out the tool with your task desires and any other desires that are related to them. Then, we're going to identify what triggers these desires and classify them as desires to be regulated upwards. This means we want to increase these positive desires so you're more motivated to tackle your tasks.

Now, here's the cool part - we're going to help you create a new and improved appraisal of your task desires. This will help you see your work in a more positive light and feel more excited to get started. But we don't stop there! We want to make sure this new appraisal becomes your automatic response, so we'll show you how to meditatively link the conditions or triggers to the new appraisal. That way, you'll be more likely to jump right into your work without any hesitation.

STOP MESSING AROUND

Serial Number	Procrastinated Task	Task Desire	Conditions/ Trigger	Why Regulate Upward	Current/ automatic appraisal	New response/ appraisal

Compelling Reason:

Chapter 6
EMOTION TOOLS

"Emotions have immense power. This power can propel you towards your dreams and goals, or sabotage and ruin your life. Choose wisely how to use the power of your emotions."
- Stan Jacobs

E**motion Tools.** Hey there! In the last section about emotions, we learned that they're pretty powerful motivators that drive us to take action. And the action we take is usually in line with the emotion we're feeling, because it makes that action seem more desirable. So, to beat procrastination, we need to flip the "desirability switch" from inaction to action or action to inaction. Remember?

But here's the thing: both the original task (that's the work we are supposed to be doing but which we are abandoning); and the alternative task (that's the thing we are doing instead) can trigger an emotion, and the one that's stronger is the one that's going to motivate you. So, if the emotion caused by the alternative task (which we called "inaction") is stronger than the one caused by the original task, you're more likely to procrastinate. And if the emotion caused by the original task (like fear or resentment) doesn't favor that task, you'll probably procrastinate too.

So, how do we stop procrastinating and make better decisions for the long run? Well, we have two tools to help us out. The first one helps you identify the emotions that usually catch you off guard, so you can deal with them before they take over. This method looks at alternative tasks as emotional triggers themselves, or as precursors to those emotional triggers.

The second tool helps you create positive emotional triggers and attach them to the tasks you want to get done. That way, you'll be more drawn to doing those tasks even if there are other things vying for your attention. And both of these tools are based on the same emotion formation process we talked about earlier, which is displayed in the diagram below. Pretty cool, huh?

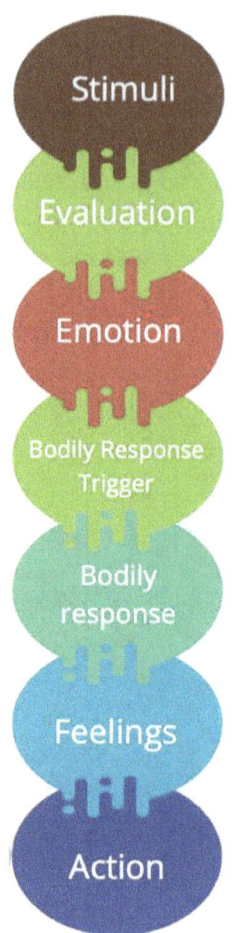

Trigger/Stimulus

Hey there, remember when we talked about emotions and how they don't just happen automatically? Well, this theory is called the cognitivist's theory and it says that our emotions go through a process of evaluation and appraisal before we feel them. So, basically, we don't just react to a situation, we think about it first and then we feel something.

Now, here's the thing, even though we might encounter the same situations as other people, we all have different thoughts and feelings about them. It's like when you and your friend watch the same movie, but you have different opinions about it. Same movie, different reactions.

So, why is this? It's because our evaluation and appraisal of a situation is unique to each of us. It's not based on our genes, but on our experiences and perspectives. That's why one person might feel scared about something while another person doesn't.

And here's another interesting fact: our responses to a situation can even change over time. So, something that used to scare you might not scare you anymore because your thoughts and feelings about it have changed.

So, there you have it! The cognitivist's theory explains how our emotions work and why we all react differently to the same situation.

Evaluation

Okay, so in the last chat we talked about the first step in emotion formation, which is stimulation. Now, it's time to move on to step number two - evaluation! This is where the magic happens, folks.

Some people don't believe that evaluation is a part of emotion formation, but I'm here to tell you that it definitely is. Basically, when we come across something that triggers an emotional response, we evaluate it to determine how we should feel and what we should do.

So, lets explain how this process works.
We encounter stimuli all the time - it could be a sound, a smell, a sight, or even a person. And depending on whether we've seen or experienced it before or not, it is classified as recognized or unrecognized. If it's something new, it passes through motivational filters and we evaluate it based on our motivations - basically, what we want or need in that moment.

Then, we store our response in our memory bank, like a library of emotional reactions. So, the next time we encounter that same stimulus, we already know how we're supposed to feel and what we're supposed to do.

It's kind of like a reflex - it happens automatically, without us even really thinking about it. But if it's a new stimulus, we have to go through the evaluation process.

So, there you have it - evaluation is a crucial part of emotion formation. And now that we understand how it works, we can start to take control of our emotional responses and not feel so helpless.

So below is a cool diagram that represents what we've just explained.

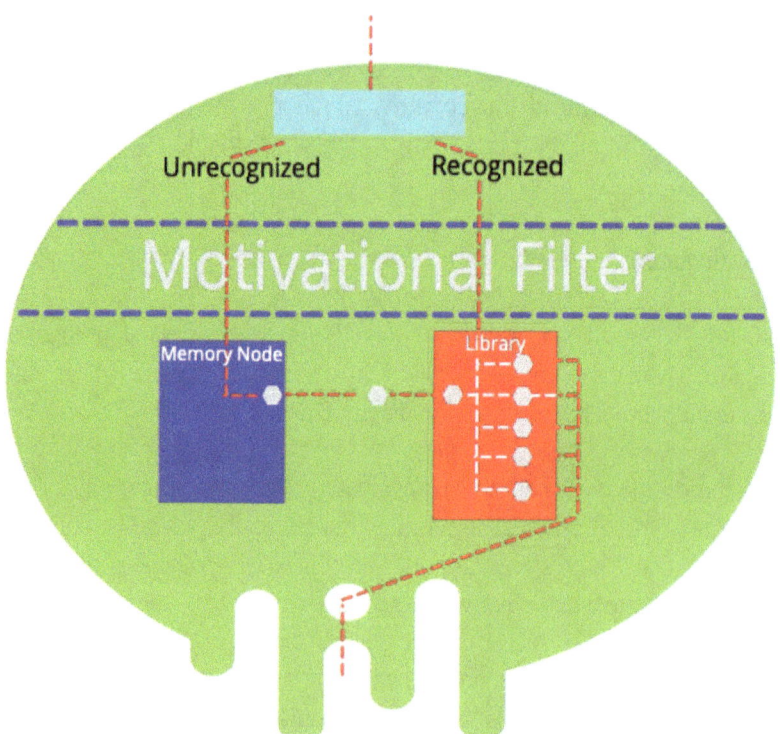

Bodily Response

Remember that we said that one of the ways we get to know an emotion has been formed is that we feel funny in our body. Your body reacts to emotions in different ways. This includes your eyes getting bigger, your skin getting conductive, your brain lighting up, your heart beating faster, and your facial expression changing. Scientists can actually measure these reactions and connect them to the cause of the emotion.[60] So, if you pay attention to your bodily reactions, you can get a clue as to what emotion you're feeling and what actions you're likely to take. That's why as we use emotion tools to tackle procrastination, we can check if they're actually working by keeping an eye on our bodily responses.

Feelings

So, emotions and feelings are a pretty cool duo. Emotions are like the first responders - they cause physical reactions like sweating or racing heart. And then feelings come in like the therapists, trying to make sense of it all.

Feelings are like the Sherlock Holmes of your brain - they start in the smart neocortical part and are shaped by your personal experiences, beliefs, memories, and thoughts. And they're super linked to the emotions they represent.

Think of feelings as the meaning your brain gives to emotions.[61] And that meaning is what fuels or determines your behavior. For example, feeling sad might make you reach for a cookie, while feeling happy might make you go for some chocolate.

And here's the thing: all feelings have actions linked to them. Some are positive, like completing projects, while others are negative, like procrastinating.

So, if you can change how, you interpret a feeling that makes you act badly, you can also change how you act. It's like playing a game of telephone with your own brain!

Behavior/Action

Alright, so we've talked a lot about emotions and how they affect our behavior. But let's be real, the reason you're reading this book is probably because you want to change some aspect of your behavior. And that's totally understandable! After all, your behavior is the most important thing when it comes to getting stuff done.

So, let's get to the good stuff. In the next section, we're going to introduce you to an emotion tool that's designed to help you change the way you respond to those pesky stimuli that always seem to lead to procrastination. Get excited!

Emotion Tool 1

Hey, remember that emotion trigger form you filled out in the last chapter? It's going to be super helpful for this first emotion tool we're about to introduce. So, print it out and let's get started!

This form is like a cheat sheet for understanding how emotions, feelings, and actions are all connected. It's going to help us in two big ways:

It'll make us more aware of how our emotions are influencing our behavior.

It'll help us see the sneaky ways that emotions can sneak up on us and mess with our productivity.

By using this form, we'll become way more emotionally intelligent, make better decisions, and finally kick procrastination's butt! So, grab your filled-out form, and let's compare it to the table and emotion wheel below.

Activity	Emotion Triggered	Feeling	Action
Writing Thesis	Fear	Overwhelmed	Play mobile game

The table for John will look something like the first table. Try your hands by filling out the table for the rest of our actors below.

John:

Activity	Emotion Triggered	Feeling	Action
Writing Thesis	Fear	Overwhelmed	Play mobile game

Wendy:

Activity	Emotion Triggered	Feeling	Action

Ben:

Activity	Emotion Triggered	Feeling	Action

Linda:

Activity	Emotion Triggered	Feeling	Action

Smith:

Activity	Emotion Triggered	Feeling	Action

Feelings Wheel with Action Diagram:

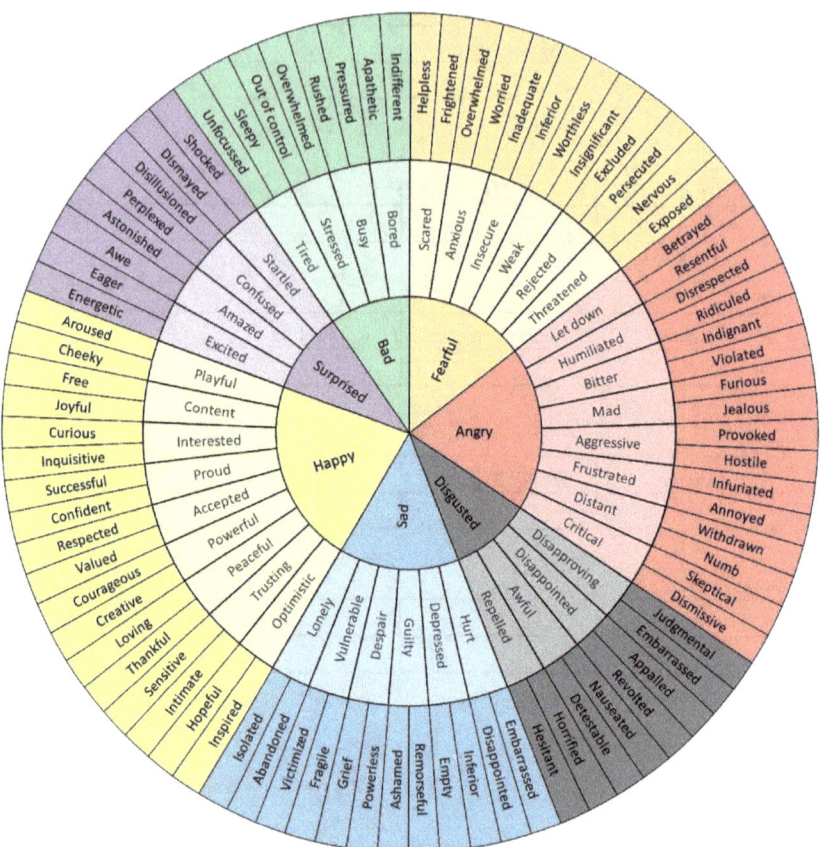

Photo via Instagram / @trainingsbyromy

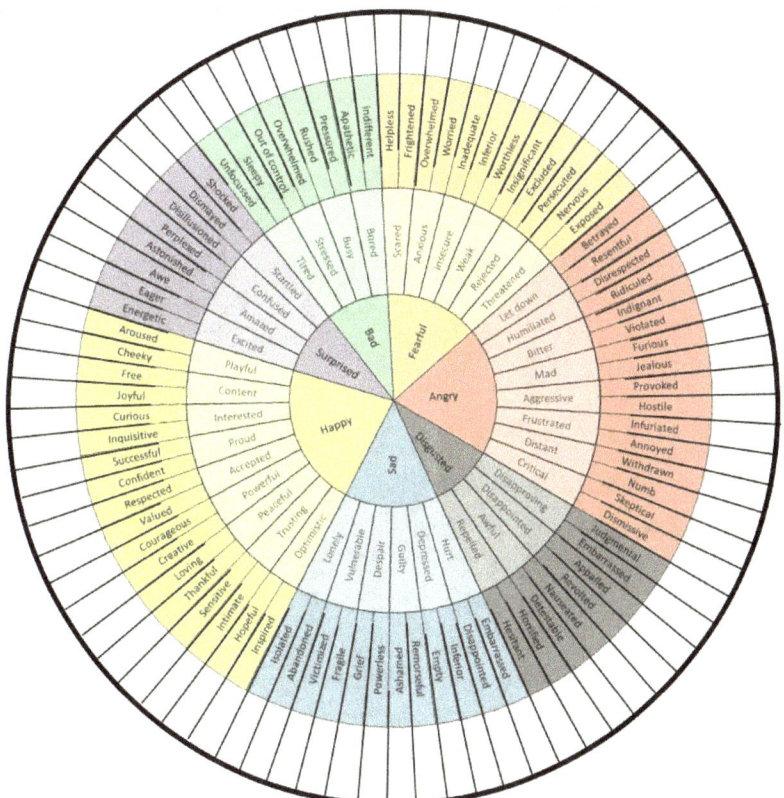

Photo via Instagram / @trainingsbyromy

Remember how we talked about emotions being lightning fast and how we usually only notice them after we've had a bodily response? Well, this tool is here to help you focus on the feelings that come after those initial bodily responses. Why? Because those feelings are what drive our actions, almost like an automatic response.

For instance, if we feel afraid, we might either run away or stand and fight. When it comes to a research project, feeling overwhelmed might make us want to give up, while feeling determined might help us push through.

By identifying how we typically react to certain emotions, we gain more control over the process. So, next time we feel that way, we can choose how we want to respond, rather than being at the mercy of our automatic reactions. It's like having a superpower!

Emotion Tool 2

Hey there! So, in this next section, we're going to show you a super cool way to turn your to-do list into a fun game that you'll actually want to play! We call it the "positive emotion trigger approach," and it's all about creating little rewards and milestones for yourself along the way to keep you motivated and on track.

See, when you're faced with a task that seems hard or boring, it's easy to get overwhelmed and just put it off. But if you can find a way to make that task, feel more enjoyable or rewarding, you'll be much more likely to actually do it. And that's exactly what we're going to do here!

So, first things first: choose a task that you've been putting off. It could be anything, from studying for a test to cleaning your room to finally writing that book you've been dreaming about. Once you've got your task in mind, it's time to break it down into smaller, more manageable pieces.

For example, let's say you want to write a book. You might break that down into chapters, and then break each chapter down into smaller sections. Once you've got your smaller pieces in mind, it's time to assign them point values.

So, for example, maybe writing the introduction is worth 50 points, and each chapter is worth 100 points. You can assign points to even smaller tasks too, like writing a certain number of pages or hitting a certain word count. The idea is to make each little milestone feel like a real accomplishment, so be sure to assign points that are challenging but achievable.

And here's the really fun part: once you've got your points assigned, you can start assigning rewards too! Maybe hitting 50 points gets you a snack and hitting 100 points gets you a movie night with friends. Keep adding bigger and better rewards as you go, so that you're always motivated to keep pushing forward.

For example:

- 50 points   - A snack
- 100 points - A movie night with friends
- 200 points - A dinner with your crush
- 250 points - A weekend hiking with your buddies
- 350 points - A PS5 game tournament
- 400 points - That tablet you've been crushing on.
- 500 points - A vacation

You can even turn it into a little game, challenging yourself to beat your own records or seeing how quickly you can hit each milestone. The key is to make it fun and rewarding, so that you actually look forward to doing the work. And who knows? You might even find that you enjoy the task more than you thought you would!

Alrighty, champ! Check out this table I made just for you! Give it a whirl and try out your own task. Let's see if you can make it rain points and rewards like a pro. Good luck, you got this!

Task	Total points

Alrighty, so we talked about how to make boring tasks more fun and engaging, and we came up with two ways to do that. The first way was to break the task down into mini-goals and reward yourself along the way. The second way is to remind yourself why you actually wanted to do this task in the first place! Maybe you picked it because it seemed interesting, or maybe you enjoy the challenge of it. Whatever it is, hold onto that feeling and let it motivate you. To help you out, we've got a handy-dandy table below. Just pick a task that usually makes you want to pull your hair out and fill in the blanks. Before you know it, you'll be looking forward to getting that task done!

Task Name:	
Why did I take on this task?	**What do I love about this task?**
Share the knowledge that has helped numerous people overcome procrastination.	It will help millions more of people to stop procrastinating

Chapter 7
Environment Tools

*You can't make positive choices for the rest of your life without an
environment that makes those choices easy, natural, and enjoyable.*
-Deepak Chopra

Environment Tool. Alright, let's talk about more tools to help you
crush your procrastination. So far, we've covered how to work
with your emotions to get you moving, but what about
environment tools? Well, that's what we'll talk about now. Instead of waiting
for triggers to set off your procrastination, we're going to take a preemptive
strike by re-engineering your environment. We'll do this by getting rid of any
negative triggers and replacing them with things that make you feel good
about getting things done.

To do this, you need to figure out what are positive and negative triggers.
Positive triggers are those things that get you excited and motivated to work
on your tasks. Negative triggers, on the other hand, are the things that push
you to avoid work and get distracted. Once you've identified these triggers,
you can start working on removing the negative ones and replacing them
with positive ones.

So, start by listing everything that makes you procrastinate and everything that helps you get work done. It can be anything, like a book that distracts you, your phone, or even your refrigerator. Then, categorize these triggers into positive, neutral, or negative. Remember, one trigger can be positive for one task but negative for another, so make sure to sort them based on each specific task.

Once you've got your list sorted, start by removing the negative triggers and adding in the positive ones. If there are neutral triggers, figure out what to do with them. After that, you can color code your workspace, create a gadget home for your devices - a box where you can lock away gadgets that distract you, and create opportunities for movement without distractions. These are all steps that can help you re-engineer your environment and boost your productivity.

So, let's track your progress in re-engineering your environment with these table below. Let's get to work!

Task:		
Positive Trigger	Neutral Trigger	Negative Trigger
ERGONOMICS		
Color Code	Gadget Home	Space

Chapter 8
Pleasurableness Tools

"Success is not the key to happiness. Happiness is the key to success. If you love what you are doing, you will be successful."
- Albert Schweitzer

Pleasurableness Tool. So, we've talked about how pleasure plays a big role in whether we choose to procrastinate or not. Our pleasure tools aim to make action more desirable than inaction by changing how much pleasure we get from each option. But how can we do that? Well, it all comes down to our perception - how we understand and interpret things around us.

Perception is a fancy word for the way we see things. It's like putting on a pair of glasses that helps us make sense of the world. And just like glasses, our perception can be adjusted to give us a clearer or fuzzier picture.

So how do we adjust our perception? It all starts with three steps: selection, organization, and interpretation.[62] First, we select which stimuli (aka things around us) to pay attention to. We usually focus on the things that are intense, repetitive, unusual, or unexpected - basically, anything that stands out. Next, we organize the information we receive by categorizing it based on our experiences and knowledge. Finally, we interpret what the information means to us based on our beliefs, expectations, emotions, and motivation.

Since perception is mostly a cognitive process (meaning it's all in our heads), we can consciously influence it. By changing how we perceive things, we can change our behavior and response to different stimuli.[63] So, if we want to stop procrastinating and start taking action, we can try changing how we perceive the things that are keeping us from doing what we need to do.

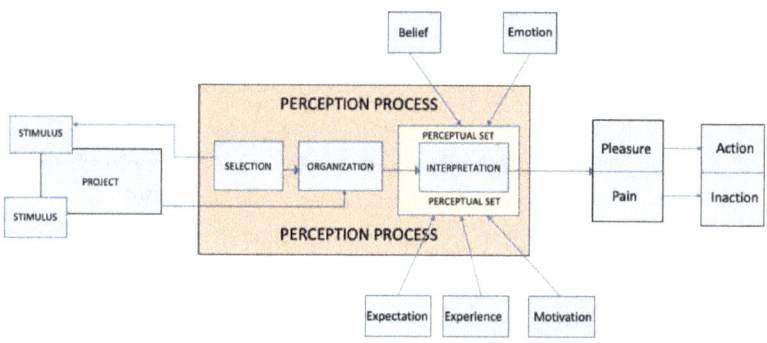

The Perception process.

Hey, teens! We just talked about how pleasure affects our actions, right? Well, now we're going to get into the nitty-gritty of how our brains perceive things and decide whether to procrastinate or take action.

To do this we will use the fancy diagram above to explain the process. First things first, there are three steps to the perception process: selection, organization, and interpretation. Let's break it down.

Selection: When we encounter a task or project, there are a bunch of different things that could be enticing us to take action or put it off. It could be our passion for the project, the consequences of not doing it, or the sweet rewards we'll get from completing it. One of these stimuli is going to stand out above the others and that's the one we focus on and therefore select.[64]

Organization: Once we've selected our stimulus, we start to organize the information it's giving us. We categorize it based on physical appearance, social role, social behavior, and our own psychological disposition.[65,66]

Interpretation: This is where things get interesting. We interpret the information we've categorized based on our perceptual set. That's basically our predisposition to see things a certain way based on our past experiences, beliefs, and emotions.

Now, if we want to change our actions or behavior, we have to mess with the perception process a bit. That means we need to focus on the selection and interpretation stages.

Pleasurableness Tool 1

Okay, so when you're about to start a project, there's always one thing that really gets you going - that's the dominant stimulus. And which one you choose will determine whether you're going to actually do the thing or just procrastinate. Usually, we don't even think about which stimulus we're selecting - it just kind of happens automatically.67 But with this cool tool, you can actually make a conscious decision about which stimulus to go for. It'll
help you pick the right one every time you start a task. The most common stimuli are consequences, outcomes/results, rewards, how much work it's

going to take, and your passion for the project. Take John's thesis, for example - here's what his stimuli looks like:

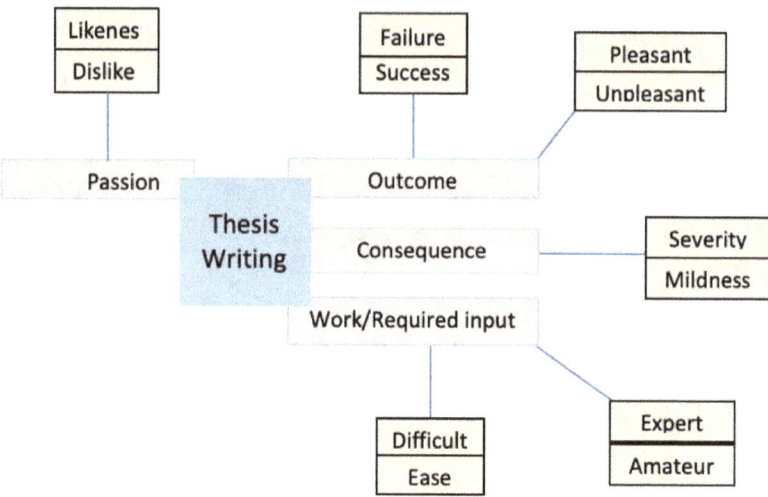

Okay, so you know John's story, right? Well, when he was faced with the daunting task of writing his thesis, he was all about the consequences. But guess what? We don't have to be like John and just let our unconscious minds choose the stimuli for us. Nope, we can take control and intentionally select the best one for the job. And how do we do that? By using the awesome diagram, we talked about earlier and filling out the form below for every task.

This way, we can choose the most positive stimulus and get ready to crush that task like a boss!

Project/Task	Stimuli	Interpretation	Perception
Project Name	Passion	Passionate:	Pleasure:
		Not Passionate:	Pain:
	Outcome	Pleasant:	Pleasure:
		Unpleasant:	Pain:
	Consequence	Mild:	Pleasure:
		Severe:	Pain:
	Work Input	Easy:	Pleasure:
		Difficult:	Pain:

So, you've filled out the form and identified the different stimuli that hit you when you encounter a task. Awesome! Now it's time to choose which one is the strongest. If it happens to be a negative one that will make you want to put off the task, don't worry. Just choose another strong and positive stimulus and concentrate on that one instead. You can use the form below to do this. Remember, you got this!

Your Name	Strongest Stimulus	My Choice Stimulus
Stimuli		
Interpretation		
Perception		

Check out John's form below, so you can have an idea of what yours could look like.

John	Strongest Stimulus	My Choice Stimulus
Stimuli	Consequence	
Interpretation	Mild: There is still enough time for m to complete the thesis.	
Perception	Mild consequence	

So, after choosing the strongest stimuli that will get you crushing the task. Focus on it and keep it in mind. You can do this by keeping this table where you can see it often and remember how important it is to crush that task.

Chapter 9
Consequence Tools

"The thing about real life is, when you do something stupid, it normally costs you..."
- Darren Shan

Consequence Tools. Alrighty, so remember how we were talking about how procrastination is the enemy of progress? Well, let's dive a little deeper into why that is. When we procrastinate, we often struggle to take action because the consequences of not doing so are in the future. It's easy to keep making excuses for not getting started because, let's face it, being lazy feels pretty good. But as the deadline creeps closer, suddenly we're able to summon the willpower to finally get moving. That's because the pain of not doing the task becomes greater than the pleasure of avoiding it.

Now, if you're a chronic procrastinator, it's probably because you're not so great at thinking about the long-term consequences of your actions.[68] It's not that you don't care about the future, it's just that you're really good at focusing on the present moment. This is what's known as your consideration of future consequences (CFC) score. Basically, the lower your CFC score, the more likely you are to put things off in favor of instant gratification.[69]

So, what can we do about this? Well, we need to create consequences that are going to make procrastinating way less appealing. But not just any consequences will do. In order for them to work, they need to meet a few key criteria:

1. They have to be unpleasant enough to make you want to avoid them.
2. They have to be enforceable.
3. They have to be applied consistently.
4. They have to take effect right away.
5. They have to get progressively more intense with each missed deadline.

And that's where our trusty form comes in. We're going to use it to create consequences that are going to kick our procrastinating butts into gear. For each consequence, we need to ask ourselves:

1. Is it nasty enough to make me want to avoid it like the plague?
2. Can it be enforced, and if so, how?
3. Will it take effect right away?
4. Will it get worse with each missed deadline?

The form will help us keep track of all the important details, like:

1. What task we're trying to tackle.
2. The benefits of completing that task.
3. The consequences of not completing it.
4. The consequences of putting it off.
5. Deadlines for different parts of the task.
6. The consequences we're going to impose on ourselves if we fail to meet those deadlines.

So, are you ready to get serious about beating procrastination? Let's do this!

Task	Benefits of Completion	Consequences of Non-Completion	Consequence of Delay	Deadline for Phases	Consequences

Okay, so let's take a peek at how John would use this form we've been talking about. He wants to write a thesis, and we're going to help him make it happen with some serious consequences for slacking off.

First, we're going to start by listing the benefits of completing the task, because let's be real, it's good to remind yourself why you're doing something when you're struggling to get started. So, John's benefits might be things like passing his class, getting his degree, impressing his professors, and feeling proud of himself.

Next, we'll list the consequences of not completing the task. These could be failing his class, not getting his degree, disappointing his professors, and feeling pretty bummed out about it all.

But wait, there's more! We're not stopping there. We're going to list the consequences of procrastinating, too. These could include things like losing sleep, feeling stressed and anxious, missing out on fun stuff, and having to scramble to finish at the last minute.

Now, we got to get more serious. We're going to set some deadlines for John to hit along the way. We'll break up the project into smaller phases and give him a deadline for each one. For example, he might have to have his research done by a certain date, his outline finished by another date, and so on.

And finally, the moment we've all been waiting for... it's time to create consequences for procrastinating. We want to make these consequences as unpleasant as possible, so John will be highly motivated to avoid them. Maybe we'll make him do 50 push-ups every time he misses a deadline or donate $20 to a political candidate he hates. Whatever it takes to get him moving!

So, there you have it, folks. John's got a plan, and it's all thanks to this handy dandy form. Will it work? Only time will tell, but we've got high hopes for our boy.

Task	Benefits of Completion	Consequences of Non-Completion	Consequence of Delay	Deadline for Phases	Consequences
Thesis	- Graduation - Feel good - Respect	- Fail course - Non-graduation - Shame	- Poor result	- Abstract - Chapter 1 - Chapter 2 - Chapter 3	- Pay James $100 for every missed deadline

CHAPTER 10
Reward Tools

"Remember: Rewards come in action, not in discussion.

- Tony Robbins

R eward Tool. Rewards are like the cherry on top of a cake, they make everything better. So, lots of cool researchers have spent time figuring out how rewards can motivate people like you and me. Two studies that are worth knowing about are:

1. Expectancy theory - this fancy idea from Victor Vroom says that how much we want to do something depends on how much we expect to get from it. So, if we're really sure that doing something will bring us big benefits, we're more likely to do it.

2. The effect of rare rewards on dopamine levels - in this study, scientists found out that when people get rewards that are better than they expected, their brains release a

happy chemical called dopamine. But when rewards are less than expected, dopamine goes away.

Our reward tool is based on these two studies. It stops procrastination by doing these two things:

1. Boosting expectancy by making the rewards we get seem bigger and more exciting. This helps us stay focused and avoid distractions.
2. Boosting dopamine levels by adding the possibility of winning a rare reward. When we win, our brains feel happy and motivated!

Shush, don't tell anyone, you've just stumbled on the treasure hidden inside this book.

Hey, hey, hey! Looks like we've got a tricky, but super fun tool on our hands here. And get this, it's going to involve not just you, but also one person that is rooting for your success! I mean, you could have more than one person that really wants you to succeed but we will make use of one of them. Okay?

Remember that letter you signed at the beginning? If you did sign it, it means you already chose that person.

So, let me break it down for you. First, you pick 5 major tasks you want to accomplish. Then, you create a list of ten cool things you would like to have as a reward for completing the 5 tasks on time. Once you've got your list ready, give it to the person you've chosen. the same person you gave the letter at the beginning. This is likely your parent, your teacher, your mentor, or whoever gave you this awesome book.

Here's the exciting part: Now, because they signed that letter at the beginning, once you finish that task within the given time, they will reward you with a surprise gift. And let me tell you, this reward could be anything - it may or may not be one of the rewards you listed, but it's definitely going to be worth it. Cha-ching! You just got yourself an accountability partner.

So, are you ready to take on this challenge with your squad and win big? Let's do this! You will use the form below for this reward tool.

Tasks:				
1.				
2.				
3.				
4.				
5.				

S/No.	Desired Rewards		Accountability Partner	Tick
1		1	Parent	
2		2	Teacher	
3		3	Mentor	
4		4	Book Donor	
5				
6				
7				
8				
9				
10				

Chapter 11
Triune-Self Tools

"Do something today that your future self will thank you for."
- Sean Patrick Flanery

Triune Tools. Let's talk about our different selves - past, present, and future! We all agree that we're not the same person we were 10 years ago, right? But when we think about who we'll be in 10 years, it's not always so clear. And that can lead to some pretty unhelpful behaviors.

Research shows that people who feel connected to their future selves are better at saving money, staying healthy, and resisting temptation. That's because they can imagine how their actions today will impact their future selves. So, if you're better at thinking about how you'll feel in the future, you're more likely to take action now to make sure your future self is happy.

But sometimes, it's hard to focus on the future. Our brains are wired to prioritize the present moment. So, when we procrastinate, we're basically choosing to make our present self, happy at the expense of our future self.

We think we'll deal with it tomorrow, but tomorrow never comes.

So, what can we do about it? Well, we have some options. First, we can take ownership of our future selves. This means getting to know that future self and thinking about what they want. We can ask ourselves questions like, "How is my future self, different from my present self?" and "Who do I want to be in the future?"

To answer these questions, we need to think about the labels we've given ourselves - things like "procrastinator" or "lazy." These labels can hold us back and prevent us from becoming the person we want to be. So, by identifying those labels and letting go of them, we can start to transform into our future selves.

Take Ownership of Your Future Self

Ready to take ownership of your future self? Take the questionnaire below and fill out the form that follows to get started!

1. What does my future-self want?
   - List three things your future-self wants to achieve or have in the next 5-10 years.
     1.
     2.
     3.
2. How does my future-self differ from my past and present selves?
   - Identify three key differences between your past, present, and future selves.
     1.
     2.
     3.
3. Who should my present-self be to align with my future-self?
   - List three qualities or habits you must adopt to align your present-self with your future-self.
     1.
     2.
     3.
4. What are the goals and values of my future-self?
   - List three goals and values of my future-self.
     1.
     2.
     3.
5. What steps do I need to take to align my present-self with my future-self?
   - List three steps you need to take to align your present-self with your future-self
     1.
     2.
     3.
6. What obstacles might I face in achieving my future-self and how can I overcome them?
   - List three obstacles you might face in achieving your future-self and how you can overcome them
     1.
     2.
     3.
7. How can I hold myself accountable for achieving my future-self?
   - List three ways you can hold yourself accountable for achieving your future-self
     1.
     2.
     3.

Answering these questions will help you gain a clearer understanding of your future-self and what you need to do to align your present-self with that vision. It will also help you identify any obstacles that might prevent you from achieving your goals and develop strategies to overcome them.

Remember, taking ownership of your future-self is a continuous process that requires regular reflection and adjustment. By regularly checking in with yourself and aligning your present-self with your future-self, you can create a fulfilling and purposeful life that meets your long-term goals and values.

Hey there, future superstars! So, you know who you are now, and you've even got an idea of who you want to be in the future. But, to really take charge of your destiny, you need to understand how your future self is different from your past and present selves. Remember those labels you gave yourself before? Well, now it's time to picture your future self and come up with new labels that will accurately describe who you want to be. Are they different from your current labels? How so? Once you've got this down, the next step is to ask yourself: "What can I do to drop my present-self labels and pick up those of my future-self?" This will help you take action and move towards becoming the awesome person you want to be!

Old labels	Description of my Future-self	New Labels	What do I do to drop old labels

Realize and Implement the Democracy of Self

You have now met your present and future selves. let me introduce you to the concept of democracy of self! Basically, it means you have to recognize that your present and future selves are different entities. I know, mind-blowing, right? But seriously, if you want to make sure you're making decisions that won't come back to bite you later, you have to listen to all versions of yourself.

So, imagine you're deciding whether to study or procrastinate on TikTok. Your present-self is probably all like "woohoo, procrastination party!" But what about your past-self? Can they tell you from their experience that maybe studying would be a better idea? And what about your future-self? What do they want?

By putting all versions of yourself to a vote, you can make decisions that are fair to everyone. And get this, you're already doing it subconsciously! But by consciously practicing democracy-of-self, you'll get better at it, and it'll become second nature.

So, next time you're faced with a decision, ask yourself: what does my past-self say? What does my future-self want? And what does my present-self think? You might be surprised at how much they all have to say. Remember, democracy isn't just for politics - it's for your own mind too!

Hold Regular Round Table Meetings of Yourselves

Hey, fellow habit-forming teens! Habits are like our brains' personal assistants - they make our lives easier by automating decisions we make repeatedly. And that's where democracy-of-self comes in - it helps us make those decisions with all versions of ourselves in mind.

But listen up, if you want to make sure your future-self is always the boss, you have to make it a habit. That means scheduling regular meetings between your past-self, present-self, and future-self (kind of like a time-traveling board meeting).

During these meetings, you'll appraise recent decisions and figure out which version of yourself won out. Then, you have to make sure your future-self's interests take priority in decisions yet to be made. Easy peasy, lemon squeezy.

But what about those spur-of-the-moment decisions? Like when you're tempted to put off studying and binge-watch Netflix instead? That's where visualization comes in. Imagine your future-self, looking all successful and proud, and ask yourself what they would do in that moment. Trust me, they're not going to let you slack off.

And by doing this regularly, it'll become second nature to put your future-self first. So, let's make democracy-of-self a habit, shall we? And who knows, maybe we'll even get our brains their own little suits and ties for those time-traveling board meetings.

Topic:				
What Past-Self says	What Present Self says	What Future-self says	Who won	Why

.

Chapter 12
Prioritization Tools

"Today's priorities should be reflective of tomorrow's regrets that you don't want."
- Germany Kent

Prioritization Tools. Picture this: you wake up in the morning, and you have no idea what to do first. So, you scroll through your phone or stare blankly at the wall, and before you know it, it's already noon, and you haven't accomplished anything. We've all been there, and it's not a fun place to be. It's like being lost in a maze with no idea which way to turn. Just like Alice in Wonderland, who didn't care where she was going, and ended up nowhere.

But fear not, my friend! The key to avoiding this trap is to know where you're headed. You can't get to your destination if you don't know where it is. And the same goes for tasks. If you don't know what you need to do, you'll end up doing nothing or doing the wrong thing. That's why prioritization is essential.

But let's be real, it's hard to prioritize when you have a million things going on in your head. It's like having a mental juggling act, and you're not sure which ball to catch first. That's why it's crucial to have a list. Write down all the tasks that you need to do and then rearrange them in order of importance. You can use post-it notes, set it as your computer wallpaper or phone screensaver, or put it on a whiteboard in your room. Whatever works for you! The key is to have it somewhere visible so that you can refer to it easily.

Trust me, once you start prioritizing your tasks, everything becomes more manageable. You'll know exactly what you need to do, and when you need to do it. No more aimlessly wandering around like Alice in Wonderland. So go ahead, grab a pen and paper, and start making that list. Your future self will thank you for it!

My Tasks for: Day.............	
1	
2	
3	
4	
5	
6	
7	
8	
9	
10	

Conclusion

Hey, you deserve a high-five for making it this far! In today's world of short attention spans, it's no easy feat to consume the content of a book for over six hours. But hold up, we're not just celebrating your progress. We're also counting on you to take action and make it count. You've got this! You can do it by committing to applying the same formula that has worked for others and actually putting it into practice. Remember, it's not just about what you know, it's about what you do with that knowledge. So, let's go! See you at the top!

ABOUT THE AUTHOR

M.G David is a seasoned banking professional with over 24 years of experience in the industry. He has risen through the ranks to hold senior executive positions at some of the world's largest financial institutions. His wealth of knowledge and expertise in the business and finance world has made him a sought-after speaker and consultant.

In addition to his extensive experience in the banking industry, M.G David holds a Masters in Business Administration from EBS and a Masters in Software Engineering from the University of Liverpool. These qualifications have further equipped him with a broad understanding of business and technology, allowing him to offer valuable insights and perspectives to his clients and readers. With his diverse background, M.G David is able to approach personal development from a holistic viewpoint, taking into account both the business and technical aspects of growth and success.

What sets M.G David apart is his ability to communicate complex concepts in a way that is both engaging and easy to understand. He has a talent for breaking down even the toughest subjects into simple, actionable steps that anyone can follow. His writing is clear, concise, and packed with practical advice that readers can apply to their own lives.

M.G David's passion for educating and empowering others to take control of their personal development has earned him a dedicated following. His book has received rave reviews, with readers praising his unique approach to motivation. M.G David's commitment to making actionable personal development tools accessible to everyone has made him a trusted authority in the industry and a true champion

.

END NOTES

Hey there, my teen friend! Have you ever read a book or a research paper and noticed some tiny numbers at the end of some of the pages? Well, those little numbers are called "end notes."

End notes are like little side notes that provide additional information or clarification about something in the main text. They can be used to give credit to sources, explain complex ideas, or simply provide interesting facts.

Think of end notes like the bonus features on a DVD or Blu-ray disc. You know how you can watch the movie and then go back to watch the director's commentary or behind-the-scenes footage? That's kind of like what end notes are for a book or research paper. They give you extra insight and information that you might find interesting or helpful.

Now, you might be thinking, "Why don't they just put all that extra info in the main text?" Well, sometimes the main text can get too long and complex, so it's easier to put extra information at the end. Plus, some people might not be interested in all the extra details, so they can just skip over the end notes if they want.

So, there you have it, my friend! End notes are like little Easter eggs in a book or research paper that can provide extra information or clarification. Who knows, you might just learn something cool if you take the time to read them!

1. American Time Use Survey — 2021 Results. (2022, June 23). In https://www.bls.gov/ (USDL-22-1261). Bureau of Labor Statistics. US Department of Labor. Retrieved March 15, 2023, from https://www.bls.gov/news.release/pdf/atus.pdf.

2. Procrastination, A Modern-day Plague. (n.d.). Procrastination, a Modern-day Plague. https://www.corporatewellnessmagazine.com/article/ procrastination -a-modern-day-plague

3. Vaden, R. V. (2012, March 19). Is Procrastination Killing You and Your Company? Author Offers Proven Distraction Busters. CNBC. Retrieved March   15, 2023, from https://www.cnbc.com/2012/03/19/is-procrastination-killing-you-and-your-company-author-offers-proven-distraction-busters.html

4. Abbasi, I. S., & Alghamdi, N. G. (2015). The prevalence, predictors, causes,   treatment, and implications of procrastination behaviors in general, academic, and work setting. International Journal of Psychological Studies, 7(1), 59-66.

5. Better Get to Work: Procrastination May Harm Heart Health. (2015, May 5). Association for Psychological Science - APS. https://www.psychologicalscience.org/news/minds-business/better-get-to-work-procrastination-may-harm-heart-health.html

6. Hesiod, Works and Days, line 405. (n.d.). Hesiod, Works and Days, Line 405. https://www.perseus.tufts.edu/hopper/ text?doc=Perseus%3Atext%3A1999.01.0132%3Acard%3D405

7.   Aurelius, M. (2020, September 13). Meditations - Marcus Aurelius: Annotated.

8.   Thucydides: The Outbreak of the Peloponnesian War (432 B.C.). (n.d.). Thucydides: The Outbreak of the Peloponnesian War (432 B.C.). http://www.thelatinlibrary.com/imperialism/readings/thucydides 1.html

9.   Cicero, M. T. (2012, March 1). The Orations of Marcus Tullius Cicero, Tr by C D Yonge.

10.   Kasper, G. (2004, March 30). Tax procrastination: Survey finds 29% have yet to begin taxes. Retrieved March 14, 2006, from http://www.prweb.com/releases/2004/3/prweb114250.htm

11.   MIT News Office, P. D. (2012, August 3). Study: Many Americans   die with virtually no financial assets.' MIT News | Massachusetts Institute of Technology. https://news.mit.edu/2012/end-of-life-financial-study-0803

12.   Johann Rall, Defended british colonial interests in north America, Battle of   trenton staged in secret, Colonial victory at trenton becomes rall's legacy, Books. (n.d.). Johann Rall, Defended British Colonial Interests in North America, Battle of Trenton Staged in Secret, Colonial Victory at Trenton Becomes Rall's Legacy, Books. https://reference.jrank.org/biography-2/Rall_Johann.html

13.   B., G. (n.d.). George B. McClellan. American Battlefield Trust.https://www.battlefields.org/learn/biographies/george-b-mcclellan

14.   How The Mona Lisa and These 4 Famous Artworks Were Never Finished? (2021, June 12). TheCollector. https://www.thecollector.com/how-mona-lisa-and-famous-artworks-were-never-finished/

15.   SHERIDAN, Richard Brinsley (1751-1816), of no fixed address. History of   Parliament Online. (n.d.). SHERIDAN, Richard Brinsley (1751-1816), of No   Fixed Address. | History of Parliament Online. https://www.historyofparliamentonline.org/volume/1790-1820/member/sheridan-richard-brinsley-1751-1816

16.   Barrère, J. (2023, February 22). Victor Hugo. Encyclopedia Britannica.   https://www.britannica.com/biography/Victor-Hugo

17.   Britannica, T. Editors of Encyclopedia (2023, March 7). Douglas Adams.   Encyclopedia Britannica. https://www.britannica.com/biography/Douglas-Adams

18.   Rambler #134, by Samuel Johnson. (n.d.). Rambler #134, by Samuel Johnson. https://www.samueljohnson.com/ram134.html

19.   #MARM: Margaret Atwood Reading Month 2022. (2022, November 28). #MARM: Margaret Atwood Reading Month 2022 – Consumed by Ink. https://consumedbyink.ca/2022/11/28/marm-margaret-atwood-reading-month-2022/

20.   A quote by Margaret Atwood. (n.d.). Quote by Margaret Atwood: "If I Waited for Perfection, I Would Never Write. . ." https://www.goodreads.com/quotes/286034-if-i-waited-for-perfection-i-   would-never-write-a

21.   Arad. A, Feige. K(Producers), Favreau.J (Director). (2010). Ironman 2 [Motion Picture]. United States. Marvel Studios.

22.   Procrastination Is the Perfect Art of Inaction. (2023, March 1). Psychology Today. https://www.psychologytoday.com/us/blog/escaping-our-mental-traps/202206/procrastination-is-the-perfect-art-inaction.

23.   Cunff, A. L. L. (2019, July 26). Why we wait: the neuroscience of procrastination. Ness Labs. https://nesslabs.com/neuroscience-of-procrastination

24.   Cunff, A. L. L. (2019, July 26). Why we wait: the neuroscience of procrastination. Ness Labs. https://nesslabs.com/neuroscience-of-procrastination

25.   Zhang, W., Wang, X., & Feng, T. (2016). Identifying the neural substrates of procrastination: A resting-state fMRI study. Scientific reports, 6(1), 1-7.

26.   Michałowski, J.M., Wiwatowska, E. & Weymar, M. Brain potentials reveal reduced attention and error-processing during a monetary Go/No-Go task in procrastination. Sci Rep 10, 19678 (2020). https://doi.org/10.1038/s41598-020-75311-2

27. Rabin, Laura & Fogel, Joshua & Eskine, Kate. (2010). Academic procrastination in college students: The role of self-reported executive function. Journal of clinical and experimental neuropsychology. 33. 344-57. 10.1080/13803395.2010.518597.

28. Wiesner, J.L. Mental freedom: Who has control-the rider or the horse? Int. J. Dharma Studies 2, 7 (2014). https://doi.org/10.1186/s40613-014-0007-829.

29. Hershfield H. E. (2011). Future self-continuity: how conceptions of the future self transform intertemporal choice. Annals of the New York Academy of Sciences, 1235, 30–43. https://doi.org/10.1111/j.1749-6632.2011.06201.x 30.

30. Alvarez, M. (2017). Are Character Traits Dispositions? Royal Institute of   Philosophy Supplement, 80, 69-86. doi:10.1017/S1358246117000029

31. Yunus, M. R. B. M., Wahab, N. B. A., Ismail, M. S., & Othman, M. S. (2018). The Importance Role of Personality Trait. International Journal of Academic Research in Business and Social Sciences, 8(7), 1028–1036.

32. Big Five Personality Traits: The 5-Factor Model of Personality. (2022,   November 3). Study Guides for Psychology Students - Simply Psychology. https://simplypsychology.org/big-five-personality.html

33.   Big Five personality traits predicting active procrastination at work: When self- and supervisor-ratings tell different stories. (2022, June 10). Big Five Personality Traits Predicting Active Procrastination at Work: When Self- and Supervisor-ratings Tell Different Stories - ScienceDirect. https://doi.org/10.1016/j.jrp.2022.104261

34.   Big Five personality traits predicting active procrastination at work: When self- and supervisor-ratings tell different stories. (2022, June 10). Big Five Personality Traits Predicting Active Procrastination at Work: When Self- and Supervisor-ratings Tell Different Stories - ScienceDirect. https://doi.org/10.1016/j.jrp.2022.104261

35.   University of Warwick. (2014, September 9). Students take note: Evidence that leaving essays to the last minute ruins your grades. ScienceDaily. Retrieved March 15, 2023 from www.sciencedaily.com/releases/2014/09/140909144542.htm

36.   University College London. (2017, February 21). Humans are hard-wired   to follow the path of least resistance. ScienceDaily. Retrieved December 11, 2022, from www.sciencedaily.com/releases/2017/02/170221101016.htm

37.   What's the Difference Between an Emotion and a Desire? (2023, March 1). Psychology Today. https://www.psychologytoday.com/us/blog/hide-and-seek/201603/whats-the-difference-between-emotion-and-desire

38.   Morse. (2006, January 1). Decisions and Desire. Harvard Business Review. Retrieved   December 11, 2022, from https://hbr.org/2006/01/decisions-and-desire

39.   Burton. (2022, November 1). What's the Difference Between an Emotion and a Desire? Psychology Today. Retrieved December 12, 2022, from https://www.psychologytoday.com/us/blog/hide-and-seek/201603/whats-the-difference-   between-emotion-and-desire

40.   What's the Difference Between an Emotion and a Desire? (2023, March 1). Psychology Today. https://www.psychologytoday.com/us/blog/hide-and-seek/201603/whats-the-difference-between-emotion-and-desire.

41.   When thought suppression backfires: its moderator effect on eating psychopathology - PubMed. (2015, September 1). PubMed. https://doi.org/10.1007/s40519-015-0180-5

42.   Bechara A. (2004). The role of emotion in decision-making: evidence from neurological patients with orbitofrontal damage. Brain and cognition, 55(1),   30–40 https://doi.org/10.1016/j.bandc.2003.04.001

43.   Karimova, H. K. (2017, December 24). The Emotion Wheel: What It Is and How to Use It. PositivePsychology.com. Retrieved December 12, 2022, from https://positivepsychology.com/emotion-wheel/

44.   What Happens During Fight or Flight Response. (2019,
        December 09). Retrieved from
        https://health.clevelandclinic.org/what-happens-to-your-body-
        during-the-fight-or-flight-response/

45.   Zohar, A. H., Shimone, L. P., & Hen, M. (2019). Active and
        passive procrastination in terms of temperament and character.
        PeerJ, 7, e6988. https://doi.org/10.7717/peerj.6988

46.   Romocean, M. (2017, December 12). The Psychological Impact
        of Light & Color | TCP Lighting Solutions. TCP Lighting.
        Retrieved December 12, 2022,   from
        https://www.tcpi.com/psychological-impact-light-color/.

47.   HOW LIGHTING AFFECTS THE PRODUCTIVITY OF
        YOUR WORKERS. (2017, September 11). UNC-MBA.
        https://onlinemba.unc.edu/news/how-lighting- affects-
        productivity/

48.   Stewart, P.C., Goss, E. Plate shape and colour interact to
        influence taste and   quality judgments. Flavour 2, 27 (2013).
        https://doi.org/10.1186/2044-7248-2-27

49.   Romocean, M. (2017, December 12). The Psychological Impact
        of Light & Color | TCP Lighting Solutions. TCP Lighting.
        Retrieved December 12, 2022, from
        https://www.tcpi.com/psychological-impact-light-color/

50.   Romocean, M. (2017, December 12). The Psychological Impact of Light & Color | TCP Lighting Solutions. TCP Lighting. https://www.tcpi.com/psychological-impact-light-color/

51.   Ćurčić, A., Kekovic, A., Ranđelović, D., & Momcilovic-Petronijevic, A. (2019). Effects of color in interior design. Zbornik radova Građevinskog fakulteta, 35, 867-877.

52.   How Cultural Differences Shape Your Happiness. (n.d.). Greater Good. https://greatergood.berkeley.edu/article/item/how_cultural_di fferences_shap e_your_happiness

53.   Are You Social and Spontaneous? You Might Be an ESFP. (2022, September 27). Verywell Mind. https://www.verywellmind.com/esfp-extraverted-sensing-feeling-perceiving-2795984

54.   O'Keefe, P. A., Dweck, C. S., & Walton, G. M. (2018). Implicit theories of interest: Finding your passion or developing it?. Psychological science, 29(10), 1653-1664.

55.   Hershfield, H. E. (2011). Future self-continuity: How conceptions of the future self transform intertemporal choice. Annals of the New York Academy of Sciences, 1235(1), 30-43.

56.   Vohs, K. D. (2015). Desire and desire regulation. The psychology of desire, 61.

57.   Hofmann, W., & Kotabe, H. P. (2014). Desire and desire regulation: Basic processes and individual differences.

58.   5 Elements of Desire Formation. (2023, March 1). Psychology Today. https://www.psychologytoday.com/us/blog/science-choice/201610/5-elements-desire-formation

59.   Watts, T. W., Duncan, G. J., & Quan, H. (2018). Revisiting the Marshmallow Test: A Conceptual Replication Investigating Links Between Early Delay of Gratification and Later Outcomes. Psychological science, 29(7), 1159–1177. https://doi.org/10.1177/0956797618761661

60.   Doorley, J.D., Kashdan, T.B. Positive and Negative Emotion Regulation in College Athletes: A Preliminary Exploration of Daily Savoring, Acceptance, and Cognitive Reappraisal. Cogn Ther Res 45, 598–613 (2021). https://doi.org/10.1007/s10608-020-10202-4

61.   Tynan, S. A. (2014). Inhibitory control and classroom behavior in kindergarten children.59. Perspective - Definition, Meaning & Synonyms. (n.d.). Vocabulary.com. https://www.vocabulary.com/dictionary/perspective

62.   Bergstrom, J.R, Duda, S. , Hawkins, D. & McGill, M. (2014) 4 -Physiological Response Measurements,Pages 81-108, ISBN 9780124081383, https://doi.org/10.1016/B978-0-12-408138-3.00004-2.

63.   Feeling Our Emotions. (n.d.). Scientific American. https://doi.org/10.1038/scientificamericanmind0405-14

64. Schweizer, K., & Koch, W. (2003). Perceptual processes and cognitive ability. Intelligence, 31(3), 211-235.

65. Schweizer, K., & Koch, W. (2003). Perceptual processes and cognitive ability. Intelligence, 31(3), 211-235.

66. Adler, R. B., Rosenfeld, L. B., & Proctor II, R. F. (2020, November 16). Adler: Interplay: The Process of Interpersonal Communication.

67. 67. Krisst, L., Montemayor, C., & Morsella, E. (2015, October 1). Deconstructing Voluntary Action. The Sense of Agency, 25–62. https://doi.org/10.1093/acprof:oso/9780190267278.003.0002

68. Dunn, K. (2013, March 23). Why Wait? The Influence of Academic Self-Regulation, Intrinsic Motivation, and Statistics Anxiety on Procrastination in Online Statistics. Innovative Higher Education, 39(1), 33–44. https://doi.org/10.1007/s10755-013-9256-1

69. Rebetez, M. M. L., Barsics, C., Rochat, L., D'Argembeau, A., & Van der Linden, M. (2016). Procrastination, consideration